Dare To Do It!

Nancy Rubesch

KITSAP PUBLISHING

Dare To Do It!
First edition, published 2017

By Nancy Rubesch
Cover design: Kitsap Publishing, iStock image license 91354931

Copyright © 2017, Nancy Rubesch

ISBN-13: 978-1-942661-38-2

All rights reserved. No part of this book may be reproduced or transmitted in any form or by any means, electronic or mechanical, including photocopying, recording or by any information storage and retrieval system, without written permission from the author, except for the inclusion of brief quotations in a review.

Published by Kitsap Publishing
P.O. Box 572
Poulsbo, WA 98370
www.KitsapPublishing.com

Printed in the United States of America

TD 20170310

50-10 9 8 7 6 5 4 3 2 1

DEDICATION

I wrote this book for Ed, Misha and Ian.

Contents

FOREWORD	i
INTRODUCTION	iii
EUROPE	1
AUSTRALIA	21
CHINA	41
INDIA	65
ISRAEL	99
EGYPT	113
MORE ADVENTURE	125
ACROSS NORTH AMERICA	169

FOREWORD

Seeking Adventure is a memoir of my life. Of the many journeys that Jim and I have taken, only the most memorable are included in this book. The writer, Mark Jenkins, said: "Real adventure – self-determined, self-motivated, often risky - forces you to have firsthand encounters with the world." Those are the kind of trips recounted here. With the world becoming so interdependent, it is important for people to become acquainted with other cultures, to understand other perspectives and to remove stereotypical thinking.

I wrote this book to inspire people to go out into the world and find their own adventures. When I grew up, travel was only available to the very wealthy. I had no money, but I was able to find ways to travel anyway. I believe that if a person wants something bad enough, he or she can find a way. One has to be proactive, and one has to be determined. There may be roadblocks, but with creative thinking these can be overcome.

The majority of the adventures that Jim and I experienced were in foreign countries, but equally important was our last trip cycling across North America. This trip was the most challenging because, by that time, both of us were in our seventies. Jim had multiple health problems, and, in fact, had just had a pace maker implanted in his chest before we left. I mention this because, as I said earlier, if one wants something bad enough he or she can find a way. We were determined to complete the four thousand mile trip under our own power. We ignored the skeptics who had stereotyped us as too old for such a trip, but we also recognized the need to make practical plans so that we could be successful. The adventure was, in fact, such a success that we hope to make another cycling trip to other parts of America.

Seeking adventure does take some courage. The traveler is confronted with the unknown. But that is what makes travel so exciting – exploring, discovering and ultimately succeeding in going out into the world, meeting the challenges and coming home a more knowledgeable and empathetic person.

INTRODUCTION

Most people like to travel, but they don't necessarily want adventure. They simply want to go from A to B. If it is done often, it becomes an automatic process – a routine that requires a minimal amount of thought. They prefer to stay within their comfort zones. But I prefer adventure because it involves much more than just traveling from one destination to another. It includes anticipating the unknown and finding oneself in a situation that could have either positive or negative results depending upon the decisions one makes. In the midst of an adventure I find my mind is engaged, my senses are heightened and I am totally involved in the event. Whatever the experience, when it is over, there is a great feeling of satisfaction.

Sometimes a simple travel plan unexpectedly turns into an adventure. For example, when Jim and I were living in Chiang Rai, Thailand, we decided to spend the day cycling in the countryside. We were told that we need only follow the road that was parallel to the river, cross a bridge at the end of the road and take the shorter route back to town. It sounded simple enough.

We started out from town following the river road, passing many small villages. Although it was extremely hot, we were able to pedal just fast enough to feel a breeze that kept us from overheating. After a while the flat road turned inward and became hilly. What had been a pleasant leisurely ride had become more challenging. At times we had to dismount and push our bikes up the increasingly steep roadway. Dripping in sweat and even feeling somewhat dizzy, I realized that Jim and I had to get out of the direct sun that was beating down on us. We had consumed all of our water and were clearly becoming dehydrated. There were trees off the road, but none close enough to give us shelter. On our slogs uphill Jim and I questioned each other about whether we should continue or turn around. We had been cycling for a couple of hours, and it seemed that we would be better forging ahead at least for a couple of more miles and hope that we would find the bridge.

Luckily, after rounding the next bend, we saw some wood railings off to one side of the road. The pavement suddenly disappeared, and only a narrow dirt lane continued in front of us. Clearly, we were at the end of the road. But it didn't matter, for we had found the bridge, and once we crossed it we would be heading back to town. We quickly dismounted and pushed our bikes up to the bridge platform. We stopped, as we looked first at the bridge and then at the swirling waters crashing against canyon walls far below us. The bridge looked like a prop for the movie, "Raiders of the Lost Ark." The sides of the structure had loose boards tacked haphazardly over gaping holes. Plywood sheets lay on the bridge deck scattered here and there presumably to cover other holes. We tentatively stepped onto the span as the bridge began to sway wildly. It moaned, groaned, creaked and grumbled. It clearly did not want us to cross. I could easily visualize the bridge falling away as we raced across it barely making it to the other side. But we were not in a movie and the person who told us the bridge was used by local cyclists must have been talking about a different structure. This did not seem safe at all.

We decided to follow the dirt lane since we could see a couple of houses in the distance. When we got closer, we saw a small cluster of buildings, but all of them appeared to be deserted. We didn't know what to do. Jim suggested we find our way to the river, which had to be fairly close. There, we might be able to flag down a boat and get a ride back up river to the town. But the single road that went in the direction of the river soon opened up into a clearing where a large house sat, shuttered against the blazing sun. We knocked on the door but no one answered. A few minutes later a lady came around the side of the house carrying a helmet. She glanced at us and nodded but then put on her helmet, mounted a motor scooter and putted up the hill. Before she actually left, we asked her to help us find transportation back to town. She said nothing, just nodded again and left. Once the noise of her motor scooter died away, there was complete silence. We didn't know what to do.

We found a water spigot, filled out water bottles and poured the cooling liquid over our heads. Even then, my face was burning and my body felt depleted of strength. We had to find a way to get back to town, but how? We sat down on a bench near a tree where there was some shade, but it was so hot we were still miserable. At least we knew that if we waited long enough maybe the lady would return and would help us then. Since we had not encountered any traffic for several hours, we knew that our chances of flagging down a car were not likely to happen. We had no phone, but then we didn't know anyone in town to call. We decided that if we rested long enough and drank enough water, maybe later in the afternoon or evening we would have the strength to cycle back to town.

But then, out of the stillness, we heard an engine being started. The driver kept working the starter until finally after several minutes the engine rumbled to life and then died. The driver repeated the process several times. Finally, the motor bellowed and then hiccupped. It didn't sound healthy. But the driver continued to step on the gas, rev the engine, which sputtered, paused for a few seconds, and then roared to life. Along with the engine noise we heard a horrible screeching of gears as they were forcefully shoved into action, and then around the corner of the narrow lane an old truck haltingly approached. A young man climbed out of the cab leaving the motor running and gestured for us to climb in the back of the truck with our bikes. Apparently he was our ride back to town. But he spoke no English; we spoke no Thai. I said, "to town," but the man didn't understand. Finally, I scratched in the dirt a rudimentary map with the logo, "Big C," the symbol for the new mall that had recently opened south of town. Immediately, the man broke into a smile and jumped into the cab, and with his foot pulsing the gas pedal to keep the motor alive, he drove us up the lane onto the paved road from which we had come.

Before we had gone a couple of miles, he pulled over to the side of the road, jumped out of the cab, and ran off. A few minutes later, he returned with a bucket of water that he poured into the radiator. He got back in the truck, and we went another couple of miles, when we stopped again while the driver went off to find water and then having brought it back, poured it in the radiator. Several times the engine died and we thought our trip was over, and then just when we were sure we would have to continue on our bikes, the fellow would get the truck started and off we would go. Several hours later, having stopped to fill the radiator with water countless times, we arrived at the mall. We had made it back to civilization, and from the mall were able to make our way to our apartment.

After a cooling shower we thought about the day's events and decided that, in deed, it was a great adventure. Maybe we were foolish to go out cycling in such hot weather. How would we know that the bike ride was much too long for two oldsters like us? Were we being too cautious in not crossing the bridge? In any case, the experience did not deter us from cycling other areas of the countryside on subsequent days.

Often times a simple excursion, such as our bike ride, became an arduous event unappreciated at the time it was experienced, but, upon reflection, would be deemed a great adventure. This was just one example of the many adventures that Jim and I shared in our many years together. But the very first adventures I experienced by myself when I was still trying to understand who I was and what I wanted out of life. One thing was for sure: I would spend my life seeking adventure.

This travel memoir describes how I was able to overcome challenging roadblocks to achieve my goal of seeing the world. In the process I learned that no matter what the dream was I could achieve it if I wanted it badly enough. It didn't matter what it was, and it didn't matter what age I was. I knew that I didn't want to wait until I was an oldster tottering about in my orthopedic shoes, wearing red hats to cover my blue rinsed perm. And I certainly did not want to be one of those persons who talked about their dreams but never followed through, and then complained in later life that it was too late. It was never too late. If I could make things happen then anyone who wanted something bad enough could find a way as well.

Perhaps I got the idea of travel from my father, who moved to Alaska to work and where I were born and lived my earliest years. He never told me why he chose to go to Alaska, in the first place, or how he picked such an incredibly wild place to live. Since he had grown up in a small mid-western town, traveling to this remote territory where the largest town was so close to the surrounding wilderness that moose and bear regularly paraded through town, was for him the greatest adventure of his life. I grew up listening to stories of his many exploits testing himself as he coped with the harsh environment. My mother would tell stories of his adventures too. She told of how worried she was when she walked to the edge of town one day and saw my father waving from the middle of the Mendenhall Glacier. She was sure he would fall into a crevasse and never be seen again. My father would just laugh and proudly tell stories of other exploits, including his search for gold. He told me once that he owned a gold mine, and to prove it, he showed me a small vial filled with tiny flakes of gold. Life was exciting for him since he could get out into nature each day. But my mother, who had grown up as a city girl, was not thrilled living in Juneau where one could walk from one end of the town to the other and be stopped by massive mountains that hovered over the houses in such a menacing manner it looked as if the huge rocky pinnacles might suddenly collapse crushing everyone and everything and push the entire population into the sea. She was anxious to return to civilization in Washington or California where she had grown up. But having listened to my father's stories for so long, I promised myself that some day I would make my life so interesting that I, too, would have great stories to tell my own children. Maybe I would also gain that confidence I needed to get by on my own in the world. Once I decided I wanted to travel and have my own adventures, I found ordinary daily routines utterly boring.

As a small child, I had access to many National Geographic magazines and the pictures of exotic cultures made me even more interested in travel. As soon as I was old enough to understand, I began reading every book I could find on anthropology and I decide that I would make it my profession.

Interestingly, when we returned to Washington state in the continental United States, my father no longer talked about Alaska as much, and over the years his stories seem to have faded from his memory. He was now settled into a routine job and was concentrating on earning enough money to pay the family bills. I don't know why he no longer talked about Alaska. Perhaps my mother had convinced him that he had to be more responsible now that he had a family to take care of. Perhaps he just saw his Alaskan adventures as part of his youth and now that he was settled in a career, he must follow the expected path through life much as his father had: going to work each day, raising a family and one day retiring. He talked about how important it was for me to get a good education and a good job. Anything related to adventure no longer seemed to interest him. If I mentioned my desire to travel the world, both my mother and he would say, "You will outgrow it." But I never did.

As I grew from childhood into my teens, my parents made it clear that when and if I were to obtain a job, I was expected to save the money for my education. If I wanted to travel I had to wait until I was out of the house, and then I would have to find a way to fund my future plans by myself. The one thing I heard over and over again from my parents was, "Don't expect anyone else to help you. If you want to do something you have only yourself to rely on."

After high school I had hoped to combine my desire to travel with a college degree in anthropology so that I could go out into the wilds, as Margaret Mead had, and study some cultural group living in some obscure part of the world. Having no money and no means to pay for my education, I was dependent on my parents for my tuition, and their plans for my future did not include anthropology or travel. Apparently I mentioned my dreams once too often, because now that I was older my parents had no tolerance for my "impossible dreams." They would angrily say, "Who do you think you are? You need to go school, get a job and stop whining about this ridiculous notion to travel."

Sometimes my parents tried to reason with me. I should be content with the life I had. Why on earth would I want to go to a strange land where the people spoke a foreign language, where people dressed and thought differently? That made no sense at all to them. Besides, they said, if I were to go to some foreign country I would undoubtedly do something stupid, and they would have to bail me out, and that, they said, they were not willing to do. I had always been so dutiful, reliable and hard working. Why did they think I was incapable of making intelligent decisions? But that was their thinking and nothing was going to change it.

Being the dutiful daughter, I followed my parents' advice and went to college so I could become a teacher. Forget the anthropology they said. With a teaching position I would always find work and I could make enough money to get out on my own. I certainly liked that idea – being on my own – since they were constantly nagging me about all the money I spent. My father would show me lists of items I had purchased that he felt were extravagant. Postage stamps, for god sakes!

There was no Internet then. I had to use the post office or a telephone to communicate in those "ancient" times. And there certainly were no cell phones. But even if there were such devices, my parents would have nixed the idea of my owning one. After all, they would say, "Who do you think you are?" There was no changing my parents' minds. No way! I was irresponsible they said. If I spent all my money on postage stamps how was I going to get by in a foreign country with foreign money and even worse, foreign people? The American way…that was where I should place my focus. I found their lack of faith in my abilities very distressing even though I knew exactly where my father was coming from. He constantly commented on how incompetent and disrespectful the younger generation was, especially females. He believed that females were expected to marry and let some man take care of them. He could not conceived of a female who might have a career in her own right, unless, of course, it was nursing or teaching, but even then, she was expected to quit work once she married, and stay home to raise a family.

When I left for college I was excited. I would finally be on my own and far away from my parents as the college was located in Ohio. I could buy all the damn postage stamps I wanted. That is, if I had a job and had some money. While my parents paid for part of my tuition, and I received money from a scholarship, I was expected to take care of my daily expenses and with only occasional part time jobs I was living very close to the edge of poverty. Despite this, I should have been happy to be away from my parents' consent criticisms.

And the funny thing is I was scared to death. Maybe it was because on the day I left, my mother, in no uncertain terms, made it clear to me that she and my father no longer had any obligations to me. They had raised me and now she said, "Go out and do your thing, but don't bring your problems back to us. We are finished with you." Whoa! Those words made me a bit anxious. I felt a panic attack coming on but managed to squelch it. Surely they didn't mean it, did they? As it turned out, they may have thought they were finished with me, but over the ensuing years I managed to give them more worries than they could possibly imagine. I guess I should be happy to know that since they did worry, it meant that they did care despite their dire words.

Nancy Rubesch

EUROPE

The first year of college was a huge adjustment. I had very little money, and when I did find temporary jobs I often was too tired from working to study and my grades took a nosedive. But by my sophomore year I had brought my grades up and obtained a temporary job that gave me enough money to pay my own tuition and even to save some money towards what I hoped would be my first adventure, a trip to Europe.

My parents thought that once I was enrolled in college I would stick to the traditional career path they had mapped out for me: education, graduation, teaching, and marriage. But they were wrong. Little did they realize that I was now enrolled in a college that attracted individuals with radical ideas. I hadn't been on campus but a few months when students took over the administration building. I don't even remember what the protest was about, but it was very exciting, and I joined in marching back and forth and thinking that I was doing something important. The police showed up and dragged the students, who were barricaded inside the main building, off to jail while the rest of us quickly scattered. The protest even made the local newspaper. I was thrilled to be part of something, whatever it was. But it was very distracting since I preferred to join the demonstrators rather than study. Fortunately, the more vocal protesters joined national groups and moved to New York City or Chicago, leaving the campus calm and quiet.

During my second year, I settled down and discovered that the classes I enjoyed the most were still those in the anthropology department. There clearly was a close correlation between my interest in world cultures and my desire to travel. I knew I had to finish my college courses, but that would take three more years. I just couldn't wait that long. And with the impatience of youth I was determined to find a way to make my dreams of travel come true right away

It seemed as if all the students I met were world travelers. They would regale me with wonderful descriptions of their adventures in Europe. I sat down and did some math, juggling expenses. Counting my meager savings in hopes of freeing up enough money to travel was not promising. I found a second job. Since I didn't think I would get to Europe any time soon, I decided to satisfy my hunger to travel by taking weekend trips to wherever I could get a ride. I would go to the student union building and read the ads stuck up on the bulletin board.

Dare To Do It!

There were always drivers wanting passengers to share the gas bill for a trip to Chicago, to New York City or Philadelphia. Those trips were only temporary fixes that were cheap enough, as I always found a student who was willing to share the floor of his/her parents' home and the parents would feed me as well. It worked wonderfully, but it didn't get me to Europe.

So how was I going to make a trip to Europe happen? I was working two jobs just to pay my basic expenses. Sometimes I was able to set aside a tiny amount for travel, but it didn't add up very quickly. And so, I decided to send away for brochures about each country in Europe that I might visit. At least I could get a vicarious thrill from reading all the material. Oh, how my father would have been angry had he known that I was using all those stamps for what he would consider a frivolous pursuit.

The college campus post office must have been wondering about all the literature that piled up in front of my mailbox. But that literature was very helpful. I learned that lots of young people hitch hiked around Europe all the time, staying in cheap hostels and eating street food. People were traveling about Europe supposedly on just five dollars a day. That sounds inexpensive in today's world, but back in the sixties, that was a significant sum of money for me. The travel brochures just made me more determined than ever to go to Europe. I decided that I would take some money from that amount I had reserved for next year's tuition, and if I slept in a hostel dorm or on a bench in a train station I could go at the end of my sophomore year. Since I had so little spending money, I planned to only visit one country. I picked Austria for one reason: enrollment in just one summer course would allow me to stay in a campus dorm for free at the University of Innsbruck. With a hot water tap and some Top Ramen I could survive

But I still had the problem of finding a cheap way to get from America to Austria. As I was reading all that literature I came across an article describing student ships that sailed from New York City to the Netherlands. All I needed was a student identification card. I applied for one at the same time I wrote requesting the forms needed to attend the University of Innsbruck and the application to purchase my passage on the ship to Europe. Once I had them filled out and sent in I was committed. The university replied with more forms to fill out, but essentially they had accepted me for that summer session. With a definite date for the class to begin I now knew the specific sailing I needed in order to arrive in the Netherlands in time to transfer to Innsbruck. As I slipped the money order for payment of the passage into the envelope I felt a few butterflies in my stomach. It was now or never. Was my dream of going to Europe really going to come true? Did I have the nerve to go? I remember my hand was shaking as I enclosed the money order, sealed the letter and then quickly shoved it into the mail slot at the post office. I had now spent enough money for the ship passage and the summer university course that I could not afford to change my mind, as the fees were nonrefundable.

Once spring quarter was finished, I went to the student union building to check the college bulletin board for someone heading to New York City. I was in luck as a graduate student told me he had just enough room to squeeze me in. Since there were five us, we would be sharing the cost of gas, making the trip very inexpensive. Since I was counting every cent, I saw this as a positive sign. My fellow passengers were interested in my plans and gave me all kinds of advice. I remember them telling me all these great ideas, but the details quickly flew out of my head as I was focused on my immediate problem, which was finding a cheap place to sleep in the city for a couple of nights before heading to New Jersey to board the ship that was going to take me on my great adventure. I did take the advice of one fellow passenger who suggested I stay at the YWCA Women's Hotel. Fortunately, the driver braved the city traffic to take me right to the front of the hotel. I barely had time to thank him and the other passengers as the driver had to double-park, and as quickly as I grabbed my luggage and was standing on the sidewalk, the car disappeared into the traffic.

The basic room at the Women's Hotel had only a bed and a window looking out at a cement wall. The bathroom facilities were down the hall. The bed was comfortable although even if it were not, I would not have noticed. I was here in New York City, and that alone was exciting enough for me to ignore any discomforts I might encounter. Luckily, the hotel had a cafeteria with food that was actually cheaper than eating at fast food restaurants. It was typical institutional fare, bland and boring, but filling.

The next day, I went outside to explore the city and was overwhelmed by the massive crowds of people rushing here and there, crowding into underground tubes, pushing and shoving. This was certainly different from the small town where my college was located. Everyone looked so sophisticated that I felt entirely out of place. I wandered about the streets sticking fairly close to my hotel afraid that if I went too far I would get lost. I remember feeling nervous. All these people were rushing here and there. None looked happy or friendly. And as I walked along looking in shop windows and trying to stay out of the way of people, I suddenly realized that I was actually going to Europe. That thought nearly took my breath away. I remember I stopped to lean against a building and take several deep breaths. This was an enormous undertaking, and I, an insignificant soul, was about to depart the safety of America and head into the unknown. Doubts flooded my mind. Who did I, a small town girl, think I was? Talking big about this great adventure and actually doing it were two different things. Maybe my parents were right after all. I should stick to the usual reliable path from college to career and forget about these impractical dreams. As I looked about I felt extremely lonely. No one seemed in the least bit interested in me. No one stopped to ask me if I were okay. Clearly no one cared.

For some reason that made no sense to me, I did the unthinkable. I called my parents. I told them I didn't think I could go. Weeks before, I had used one of those precious stamps to send them a postcard telling them I was heading for Europe. I knew they would be very worried, not about my safety, but that I would do something stupid, and they would have to bail me out. I hated myself for making that call. I had given into my fears. How could it be that my tingling toes and churning adrenal glands were not making me excited? I lectured myself: "Damn it Missie, don't be such a wimp! You have harped on travel all your life and now you must seize the opportunity." My emotions were obviously clashing with my logical reasoning.

Quaking in my shoes and angry at myself at the same time, I held the phone away from my ear when my parents answered but could still hear them saying the old refrain, "Who do you think you are?" They immediately suggested I return to my college and work through the summer and forget all this nonsense. When I hung up the phone, I stood there in the phone booth. Why had I called them? Did I secretly want them to talk me out of going? I certainly knew they disapproved of any of my travel ideas, so they naturally would not be encouraging me to go. I guess I just needed to hear them yell at me again so that it would encourage me to do just the opposite. They had no confidence in me even now after I had been living on my own at college, earning my tuition and never asking them for money. They still saw me as a spendthrift. If I gave up now I would be accepting my parents' plans for my future. I would forever think about what might have been while I worked a routine job, married and had kids just as my father expected. I thought about my father's change in behavior after leaving Alaska and how he no longer would talk about all those adventures he had had. Would I be like that if I quit now? I knew then I had to suppress my anxiety and get on that ship. I would go to Europe and I would learn to survive on my own.

The morning that I was to report to the ship, I had to travel to New Jersey and find my way to where the ship was berthed. I left early in the morning because I had no money for a taxi, and I had to ride the subway and train and then wander about asking everyone I encountered to direct me to the right place. It was a bit dodgy walking the streets near the docks, as the only people I saw were workmen, who looked rough and tough. But I managed to find the ship in time to check in and board.

I had no idea what to expect since I had never been on board a ship before. It looked fine to me except it did appear to be rather small next to the other ships tied up nearby. As soon as I walked up the gangplank and boarded the ship I was assigned a bunk in a room deep in the bowels of the ship. I clambered down several flights of stairs and finally arrived at a large room with rows of bunks separated by narrow aisles. There were four bunks on each tier, and I had been assigned a top bunk against one wall. There were no windows, which led me to believe we were below the water line. In fact, I think we might have been below the crew's quarters since I glimpsed men sitting about in a room that was a couple of flights above the room where the student bunks were. I tried not to think about the narrow corridors and the steep stairs that would be difficult to climb if everyone in the bunkroom was trying to go upstairs at the same time in an emergency.

After leaving my suitcase in the dorm, I climbed the stairs to the deck where students were talking to friends and waving to people on the dock. I waved to the crowd too just because everyone else was doing so, and it made me feel less lonely. After the ship left port, it passed the Statue of Liberty and I remember thinking that now I was actually leaving America, and it was now too late to turn back. I fell excited and anxious at the same time. By the time the crew served lunch I met several fellow travelers all going to summer school like me. They wanted to know why I choose the University of Innsbruck, and I told them I hoped to find a job and stay through the winter to ski. Of course, I knew no German so the chances of me finding a job were a bit fanciful. But I clung to the idea anyway.

From the first night on board the ship, I had to keep reminding myself that I was now living my dream even if it wasn't exactly the way I had envisioned it. Lying in the narrow bunk just inches from the ceiling and some twenty feet off the metal floor, I stared into the darkness clutching the edges of the bunk to keep from falling off, as the ship heaved back and forth. There was no way I could sleep when the ship tipped so far to one side or the other that the floor appeared almost vertical.

It was bad enough rolling back and forth on my bunk, but then someone turned on the light, and I looked up to see hundreds, probably thousands, of cockroaches scrambling about the ceiling only a couple of feet from my face.

If I weren't eaten by roaches – they eat everything, right? – I was sure the ship was going to sink. I clambered out of my bunk, down the ladder and crawled, as if drunk, through the narrow corridor, up the stairs on all fours and out onto the deck. For the next five nights I slept in a deck chair, freezing my hind end off and watching the water splash over the railing and believing that just one more wave, and the whole ship was going down. But the thought of going back down in that hole and staring at cockroaches was just too revolting.

But things were not all bad. A day after boarding the ship, I had met and made friends with a number of young people, like myself, who were excited about going to Europe. I tried to quell the anxiety I felt being on a ship that rolled so much. Everyone said the weather was fine and the rock and rolling was natural, but I could feel my stomach doing flip-flops, and at times my head hurt as if a heavy weight had burrowed into my forehead just above my eyes. As I got to know different students I was impressed by their confident manners. But listening to them I discovered that most of them had gone to Europe in the past with their parents so, although they were going alone on this trip, they were used to travel, and since most of them were with friends, this trip did not bother them.

After a week of rocking and rolling with the waves that made me feel constantly queasy I was thrilled to see the port of Rotterdam. It was rather anticlimactic as the ship chugged ever so slowly toward the docks. It seemed to take forever for the ship to be secured, the gangplank lowered and passengers were allowed to debark. I didn't have any time to look about Rotterdam, as I wanted to go to the train station and find out when the next train would be leaving for Innsbruck. Two of my new friends and I pooled our money and found a taxi to take us to the station. After purchasing my train ticket, my friends stayed on the platform to see me off, as their train would leave later that evening. I think they also were worried about me. I may have thought I had hidden my anxiety, but they could see it oozing out of my pores and probably felt sorry for me as I was all alone while they were traveling together. I had originally planned to travel with a friend also, but she backed out at the last minute seduced by a new car her parents had given her. While I wrestled with my anxiety now that I was here in Europe and having to find my way around by myself, I wondered if my friend would do any traveling later in life or would she be happy following the usual path through college to a job and marriage and then staying home and raising a family. I know she had recently acquired a serious boyfriend, so I suspect she was more attracted to seeing him than traveling in Europe.

On the train I felt my confidence growing as I looked over all my documents for the umpteenth time. I knew where I was going, where I was to get off and where I would be staying that night. Strangers riding in the carriage with me said in their limited English that they would help me and that I was not to worry. When we arrived at the city of Innsbruck, one of my fellow travelers, a kindly older gentleman, got off the train with me and waved a station attendant over to the platform. He must have explained my situation for the attendant took my arm and led me into the train station itself. As I looked back the old man waved and then jumped back on the train just as it was leaving. The attendant, who spoke some English, said he would show me where to go and he even wrote directions to the university in German so that I would be sure to arrive safely. How kind everyone was! I may have been traveling by myself but I was never totally alone. Unlike my parents' distrust of foreigners, I found these people not only could be relied on but that they even went out of their way to be of help.

From that point on, I realized I could do it. I could travel about Europe, meet many interesting people and have the confidence to explore on my own. Although people spoke many foreign languages that I could not comprehend, I discovered that I could communicate through gestures and that people always wanted to help me. When I finally realized that Europeans are basically the same as Americans, I was able to relax and thoroughly enjoy my adventure. While attending the university I also had time to explore the city of Innsbruck. There were no supermarkets, but, instead, many tiny specialty shops. I quickly found bakeries with the most divine concoctions. Fortunately, I was doing a lot of walking so that eating pastries every day was not all that bad, in fact, it was delightful and better than Top Ramen!

While living in the dorm and attending the summer class in Innsbruck, I met other students from many different countries. I would have liked to know more about them, but I spoke very little German, and it appeared that the majority of the students were quite fluent. The students had enrolled in the summer program to perfect their German conversational skills, so that each day in class they talked among themselves in German while I sat in the back trying to appear to understand but was actually clueless as to their discussions. Luckily, the textbook for the course was available in both English and German so that I could understand the material enough to pass the exams. Of course, I wasn't as dedicated to the course as the other students since my whole reason for being in class was that free bed in the dorm. Students were cordial but distant appearing reluctant to speak English. They would try to talk to me in German, and when it was clear I didn't understand, they politely made excuses and quickly disappeared. It was disheartening, but my own fault. Why hadn't I taken a course in basic German or at least listened to some tapes before coming to Innsbruck? I ended up studying on my own, and when I had some free time I walked about the city. I actually enjoyed my explorations as the shopkeepers and even strangers on the street were friendly, often striking up conversations with me in English. Unlike the students at the university, ordinary persons on the street wanted to practice their English.

One day near the end of the summer session when I was thinking I would have to soon return to the United States, I ran into two Americans who were from Seattle. They were avid skiers as was I, so we struck up a conversation and soon discovered mutual acquaintances. Their friends were employees at the same ski resort where I had worked on winter weekends. The Seattle couple said that they were leaving in a few days to drive to Rome and wanted to know if I would like to accompany them. I didn't have to think twice. They said that my only expenses would be paying for a bunk at a youth hostel and finding my own meals. Since they were staying in upscale hotels and eating at fancy restaurants they were content with dropping me at hostels and meeting me later in the evening to explore. It sounded like an opportunity I could not ignore. I quickly left the university without finishing the summer course and joined the couple in their rented VW bug.

We drove to Rome, stopping in Florence to see the Duomo, one of the most famous cathedrals in Italy, the Uffizi Gallery, with its Renaissance art collection, the statue of David sculpted by Michelangelo, and Ponte Vecchio, the old bridge, often pictured in scenes of the city. I spent much of my time exploring on my own as the Seattle couple said that they had come to Europe because it was the thing to do, and once they had been to a place and had a picture taken of themselves in front of a famous site, they were ready to continue on to some other place. But they were flexible and enjoyed sitting at outdoor cafes imbibing the local brew while I spent more time exploring in depth.

We spent a week in Rome. It seemed that the Seattle couple were happy to have me along just to take pictures of the two of them posing before the Coliseum, St. Peter's Square, the Trevi Fountain and, most importantly for them, standing on the Spanish Steps with all the other tourists. I began to feel some frustration that we didn't spend more time at various famous sites, and then I reminded myself that if they had not offered to take me along with them I would never have seen any of Italy.

Not really knowing where they wanted to go next, they asked me what I would like to see. I mentioned going to Berlin, and, surprisingly, they agreed that would be a great idea. We drove north into Germany and headed for Berlin. It was 1961 and West Berlin was cut off from the rest of Germany as the land around that part of the city was being administered by the Soviet Union. Tensions were high, as the Berlin Wall had recently been built. So, driving into the city was both risky and exciting. We didn't realize how tense the Cold War had become, or we might have changed our minds about driving there. A single highway corridor was open for travelers to use, and it was completely devoid of any traffic. We were happily zipping along until we came to an intersection. We turned onto the road we thought was correct, but having no maps of the area we were just following the directions we received before setting out. We had not gone more than a half mile when several armored vehicles materialized seemingly out of nowhere. We were stopped and, with machine guns pointed directly at us, we were asked where we were going. Although the soldiers only spoke Russian it was clear from their gestures that we had veered off the main route into Berlin. It was a stomach flipping, pee in the pants moment. Having a large gun aimed directly at you by some snot-nosed youth was probably the most frightening thing I have ever encountered. Luckily, an older man came over and in halting English told us to turn around and get back on the main road. We did, and, fortunately, did not see those soldiers or any others again. When we arrived at the checkpoint to cross into West Berlin we had a similar experience with young Soviets points their machine guns directly at us. I did not have to say anything as the Seattle couple did all the talking, and that was a good thing because all I could think about was if that young man, standing in front of us, just happened to wiggle his finger, he would kill us. What a "happy" thought! I am confident that the Seattle couple was wondering why they had listened to my suggestion of driving here to Berlin. All they wanted to do was hang out in Europe, see the famous sites, and go home to tell their friends all about their "worldly" adventures. They certainly had not counted on being put in such a precarious situation. But finally we were allowed to continue on into the American sector of West Berlin.

We spent a week in the city with me acting as photographer for the American couple. I managed to visit several museums, but after visiting Italy the museum exhibits here began to look a lot like the ones I had seen before. Of course there were different artworks in the various museums, but these masterpieces required some time to digest, and I had only enough time for a cursory glance. My bored

Dare To Do It!

American couple wanted me to go with them to see some shopping area where they wanted to pose for pictures. Too bad there were no selfie sticks in those days!

Of all the places I visited in West Berlin the one structure that was most memorable was the Gedächtniskirche or Kaiser Wilhelm Memorial Church. This once grand church was bombed out during WWII leaving only a single tower standing to remind people of the horrors of that war. The other famous Berlin structure that I wanted to see was the Brandenburg Gate, but it was blocked off so that we could only view it from a great distance.

There was one event that I would remember forever whenever I think of my visit to Berlin in 1961. I went to Check Point Charlie and stood on a platform where I could look across the barbed wire fence to "No Man's Land" and into East Berlin. Directly across on the other side was a soldier standing on his own platform but with his gun pointed in my direction.

As I climbed down from the platform an American who identified himself as a newspaper reporter told me that if I were interested I could go into East Berlin. "Really? I said, "Is it a safe thing to do?" The reporter assured me that it was. I thought that it sounded like a great idea. Never mind that I didn't know this American nor did I know if he were a real reporter. So on the word of a complete stranger, I approached the guard booth on the American side. The soldiers assured me that it was safe to go across, but said that they would keep my passport as a precaution. What precaution they would not explain, but they assured me that I could get my passport back when I returned.

Without a second thought I handed over my passport and walked across "No Man's Land." I have to admit I had second thoughts about whether going over to East Berlin was a good idea. A huge sign on the pavement just pass the guard booth said, "You are leaving the American sector." I only had to walk another block, and I would be in a Communist part of the city. Ahead of me the buildings looked forlorn and deserted. Why did I want to go there when it looked so depressing? I guess I just wanted to say I had been in a communist "country."

Whatever my reasoning I continued on along the empty street stopping at the East Berlin guard booth where Russian soldiers stood in the doorway watching my approach. They were young guys all quite friendly, laughing and joking among themselves. I didn't understand anything they said but one fellow spoke some English, and he insisted that all of the soldiers had to pat me down to be sure I wasn't carrying anything into East Berlin. It would seem that one of those soldiers could have done the job, but they insisted they all had to do so. The English speaker said that it was important that they all do a search just in case. I wasn't sure what he meant by "just in case, " and his impish facial expression suggested that he wasn't entirely serious. Were they really just doing their jobs or taking advantage of a young female? I would never know!

When I arrived at the buildings in East Berlin I could see that the structures were in worse shape than they appeared from a distance. Windows were broken out, and most of the structures had damaged exteriors, either gaps in walls or broken drain pipes hanging haphazardly down from the eaves. Electric wires were dangling here and there, some tied up in unorganized loops on poles. It was clear that the buildings had been uninhabited for some time. I wondered how far I would have to walk to find anyone about or any businesses that were open. Wherever they were, it was not near the area where I was walking.

I didn't see a single person even in the distance down the long main avenue. There was no activity, no lights, nothing, just abandoned buildings. It was so depressing that I could see no reason to continue on. In fact, the place was so unsettling, I wanted to run back to the other side as quickly as I could. But as I turned around to leave, a young woman about my age waved to me from the shadows of a building. She asked me to come over and talk to her. Her English was heavily accented, but it was easy to understand her. She was very friendly, asking me where I was from and telling me how much she hoped some day to go to America. After some minutes of flattery, she got down to business. She wanted to know how much money I would take in exchange for my passport. She assured me that if I went back to the checkpoint and reported that I had lost my passport, there would be a bit of a hassle but no big deal, and I would be told to go to the American Embassy in West Berlin the next day and get a new one issued. She assured me that the old one would be destroyed immediately after being used to cross the border.

She showed me a bundle of American bills that she said totaled $1000. She went on to describe in graphic terms the sad situation of her family, all of them starving, her father ill and needing serious medical attention that could only be obtained in West Berlin. She was so good at her spiel that I was almost in tears myself. If I had had my passport, I probably would have given it to her, and that money would allow me to stay longer in Europe. It would have been a win-win situation. But when she discovered that I had no passport, she disappeared so quickly I almost wondered if I had dreamt the entire episode except that I was wide awake standing in a dreary rubble-strewn street.

As I retraced my steps to the East Berlin guard booth, an older military man approached. He asked me what I was doing, and I told him that I was just looking around but was leaving. He stared at me as if he was about to say something else, but I quickly headed to the guard booth where the soldiers were now all business. Under the watchful eyes of this older man they only gave me a cursory pat down and sent me out to re-cross "No Man's Land." When I got to the American check booth the soldiers asked me how I liked my experience, and when I told them of the young woman, who approached me with her story, they said that the event was typical. They also said that there were many young well-meaning students, who were in jail in West Berlin because they had been caught smuggling drugs. Often the money the youths received in exchange for their passports was bundled in such a way that drugs were tucked into the packages. The students would not have known about the drugs because the person giving them the money would emphasize the importance of not opening the stack of bills until they were on the other side of the border. And, of course, by then they would be stopped, searched and taken to jail.

I told my Seattle friends about my experience and they seemed somewhat interested but quickly changed the subject to discuss their own experiences sitting at some outdoor café chit chatting with fellow tourists. It seemed that the most important thing for this couple, and perhaps for other tourists as well, was to brag about their travels. I had often witnessed these exchanges when sitting with the Seattle couple in the evenings. After the initial exchange of questions about where one lived in the United States, one tourist would compare the place in Europe with his/her hometown in America. He/she would complain about European facilities that just were not up to American standards. They would give detailed accounts of traveling here or there. Then another tourist would agree that things were just substandard compared to America and then describe their own experiences visiting the same places but with some added elaboration, such as, taking a private tour with some important person who knew their third cousin on the wife's side. I found it all very boring and could only attribute this mentality to the fact that these people were all in their thirties, much older than I was at the time. I don't recall students talking this way. Students seemed so open-minded. I wondered why these tourists came to Europe if they found it all so lacking compared to the United States. But I kept out of the conversations and politely made noncommittal comments since visiting with the Seattle couple was an expected evening ritual. Of course, I took lots of photos for the couple to add to their album when they returned home. I wondered what kind of stories they would tell their friends when they were back in Seattle. Oh well, I couldn't complain. They were pleasant enough and generous to include me on their journey into Italy and now to Berlin.

Although I had been as frugal as I could, I was running out of money. I had just enough left to purchase a cheap flight to New York City. There were still many countries I would have loved to visit, but I would have to save those places for another time. I just could not find the funds to stay any longer. As it was I had traveled through most of September, and fall quarter at the college began at the end of the month. I had to get back to classes. The kindly American couple drove me to Luxembourg where the cheapest flight I could find was with Icelandic Airlines.

The flight back to New York City was uneventful, although the plane did stop in Reykjavik, but without any funds I was unable to stop over to explore the city. Once in New York I called a college friend, who found a student heading to the campus and was willing to take me along. I was back at school in no time, wondering how my adventure could be over so quickly. I was satisfied for the moment, but I knew I would want to travel again as soon as I could.

When I looked back on my short visit to Europe I realized I had learned some valuable lessons. I discovered how friendly foreigners could be and, for that matter, fellow Americans as well. I felt more confident, more mature and more positive about my own self-image. I realized that using common sense and sometimes following my gut reaction worked just fine.

Once I returned to the college campus in Ohio, I made arrangements to transfer to the University of Washington in Seattle and leave the radical college behind. I certainly had my regrets, but having spent part of my tuition money, I no longer could afford the private college. My scholarship had been used up. The cost of tuition at the University of Washington as an in-state student was about one-fourth the cost of the private college and, therefore, more affordable for me.

Using the campus bulletin board for the last time, I found a student driving to Chicago. Once in Chicago I purchase a ticket on the Greyhound bus. It didn't leave until the next morning so I spent a very uncomfortable night dozing on a bench in a rather sleazy waiting room. The bus ride was uneventful but very tiring, as it seemed the bus stopped at every station across the northern states. As people got on or off, they created enough noise to make sleeping impossible. Sometimes the bus was full of talkative travelers and other times it was relatively quiet. I remember being exhausted when I finally arrived in Seattle.

I made my way to the university student union building to find an ad for apartment sharing. Since the fall quarter was to begin within a couple of days I didn't have high hopes of finding anything, but a small handwritten note that looked as if it had been posted long before, still had a phone number I could read. When I called, the person who answered said the house was probably full, but he would consult the other renters to see if there was room to fit me in. Luckily, once I arrived at the house, I met a group of like-minded independent students who decided they could give me a small utility room off the back porch. Since it was so small, they even agreed to reduce my rent accordingly. I would have a cot and a couple of orange crates for a desk. I immediately agreed. I could not afford to continue staying at a hotel no matter how cheap. At least I had shelter for the time being, and I could then look for better arrangements in the future.

I had transferred to the University of Washington for economic reasons, but I had to admit that another reason was romantic. My boyfriend, Jim, was attending the university, and I had missed him when I was in Ohio. We had been dating on and off since we met when I was in the eighth grade. We both loved the outdoors and besides pursuing a variety of other sports activities, we had worked at a ski resort outside of Seattle. Now that I was back in the area I was able to return to my old job at the ski resort, so that every weekend I would pack up my books and head to the mountains with Jim where we both worked, skied and socialized. Somehow we were able to squeeze in some studying as well.

My basic room at the rental was good for sleeping and not much else, and that was okay because I skied on the weekends, spent my afternoons working another job I found near the university and studied all evening at the library. Life was very busy.

Eventually I graduated from the university, found a position teaching English, and married my boyfriend. Perhaps it was inevitable that I would end up in the same routine I had wanted to avoid. Within a couple of years we produced three children. I was busy preparing lessons, correcting papers, or running around to various athletic events. Jim played basketball and softball when he wasn't skiing. As the children grew, they became involved in sports as well. They all took part in competitive swimming, soccer, basketball and softball, and, of course, went with us to the ski resort where they quickly became expert skiers. Life was too busy to contemplate travel, although we did take one extensive camping trip across the northern states and up the Saint Lawrence River to the Gaspe Peninsula. It was a great way for the children to become acquainted with a different culture. Although they were young I thought the trip would be one they would remember long afterwards, but when I asked my children about the trip in later years, the only cultural thing they remember was watching *Planet of the Apes* in French in an outdoor theater and eating donuts from some home bakery in a tiny village along the Saint Lawrence River.

We were doing what young couples do, raising a family, purchasing a home and trying to put away extra money for the children's future education. Things were just as my parents had hoped, and I am sure they were happy to see me settled down and out of their hair. And I was content with the situation for a relatively long time. But after twelve years of the same routine, it was beginning to wear thin. All I could see ahead of me was the same thing day after day. I wondered to myself if this was all there was to life. It was full, and I was quite happy, but I still wanted more.

While reading a newspaper, I happened to see an article advertising teaching positions in Europe. What a great idea, I thought. This was an opportunity to break with the routine and at the same time expose the family to a different culture. This would be an educational experience too good to pass up. I wrote for the information, filled out the papers, sent them in and received an invitation to come to the university in Seattle for an interview.

After getting the family spit polished to perfection, we headed to Seattle for the big interview. When we went into the designated room we discovered it was a huge lecture hall, and it was filled with hundreds of people. There were only five positions available. It was clear that not all of these people would be chosen. I tried to keep a positive attitude when our number was called and we were ushered into a small room for the interview. We were asked a number of questions about whether we could adjust to living in a foreign country. I assured them that we could, but one of the persons doing the interviewing told us that since we had never lived abroad, we were already disqualified. One had to have had prior experience living in Europe to adequately fill one of the positions.

I was the only sad one going home. The children were too small to understand or care, and Jim was good enough to not say, "I knew you wouldn't get it." But on the way home, Jim said something that would change our lives forever, although we didn't know it at the time. He said he really wasn't interested in going to Europe. If he could go somewhere, it would be to Australia. Australia, I thought. Why that was clear on the other side of the world. It was so far away it simply seemed beyond comprehension.

Dare To Do It!

Nancy in front of the Roman Coloseum where there were few cars and even fewer tourists. The year was 1961.

The Brandenburg Gate was blocked off in 1961 to stop the people in East Berlin from trying to escape.

Checkpoint Charlie, looking at East Berlin.

1961 postcard of the Brandenburg Gate.

Dare To Do It!

Looking over the wall into East Berlin from Checkpoint Charlie.

AUSTRALIA

Several months later I saw, by chance, an ad in an educational trade magazine that the State of Victoria, Australia had an exchange program whereby teachers in Australia came to America and vise versa. Participants would receive their salaries from their own school districts but would exchange jobs taking over the classes that each had in their respective schools. I could not believe my eyes. I had to read the ad over several times. I had never considered going to Australia, but remembering Jim's comment about wanting to visit, I decided it would be worth applying to see what would happen. I wasn't particularly enthusiastic since Australia did not seem the cultural climate I had had in mind, but, on the other hand, it would be a unique experience exposing the children to a different life style.

The first step was the application. When I called to request the application form the person who answered was very enthusiastic and explained that he had been on an exchange the previous year. He said the experience was fantastic. So, when the form arrived, I filled it out and sent it back right away. I told Jim what I was doing, and he was enthusiastic. Of course, he was. He had seen how many people had applied for the teaching positions in Europe. He said he would love to go. He was sure that I would be rejected this time too. But to his surprise, and mine, we were accepted into the program. I was ecstatic. Jim looked stunned. He began to enumerate all the reasons why we couldn't go. I heard his arguments, but didn't listen. I knew that no matter how many complications, and there were many, we just had to go. Here was the opportunity to get out of the rut, that routine that I would otherwise be stuck in for the rest of my life.

I began thinking of all the other obstacles that Jim had not thought to bring up. My school district had to agree to the exchange. We had to find someone to handle our finances while we were gone. We had to store our belongings. Jim had to talk to his supervisor into giving him a year off from work. And what would we do with our dog?

I talked to the assistant superintendent in my school district, a gracious lady who had, herself, lived aboard. She was thrilled at my opportunity and gave me the go-ahead. But the principal at my high school was not happy at all. "I don't want no damn foreigner in my school," he shouted at me. And so, for many weeks prior to leaving, he would see me in the hallway at school and shout down the corridor, "You certainly have made a mess of things, Rubesch. Who do you think you are? I told you, I don't want no damn foreigner in my school."

I continued to plead my case to Jim so that in order to shut me up he went to his supervisor and asked for the year off. Here was another roadblock! The supervisor was not sympathetic and especially hated teachers. The most he would do was to allow Jim a month off to escort the children and me to Australia, and then once we were settled he had to return to work. The other problem that came up was finding a place for Jim to live when he returned to America since the Australians would be living in our house. Fortunately, he had relatives living nearby with whom he could stay.

Somehow with all the problems that faced us, I found solutions. I even talked my parents into accepting the legal power to handle our finances while we were gone. They were not happy at all to do this, but they realized that we had no one else we could trust with our money. Jim's father was deceased and his mother was in her eighties and needed someone to care for her. She was not able to handle our finances. My parents reluctantly agreed to take our dog after I pleaded with them. They had acres of land, so the dog would be able to stay with a minimum effort on their part.

We finally left for Australia right after Christmas. The Australian school year began in late January and continued through June, July and August. I would not get a summer vacation that year, but it was a trade-off worth taking.

When we arrived in Australia a lovely couple, neighbors of the Australian exchange teacher, met us at the airport and took us to the home where we would be living for the next year. Although the house was outfitted with the basic items found in any home, it was clearly more upscale than ours. It looked like something that one would see in the pages of *House Beautiful*. It was tastefully decorated with antique furniture, elegant décor and even a swimming pool in the back yard. I could hardly imagine what the Australian family must have been thinking when they walked into our modest home.

The house we would occupy for the next twelve months was many miles from stores or schools, and there was no public transportation. We had brought enough money to purchase a second-hand car, but having done that, we were broke. However, we had not been worried as my paycheck was due to arrive the same day that we took possession of the car. But the money did not come. We talked to the bank to see if there had been some mistake, but there was no record of any money transfer at all. So we asked for a loan, but the bank officials said we did not have any established credit so we did not qualify. We were, therefore, dead broke. I called my parents to find out what had happened and discovered that they had used the money from my first paycheck to pay bills due months later. Even though I had given them a detailed schedule of what bills to pay and the exact dates for payment, they had decided that, as usual, I had no financial sense and that by paying several months in advance they were freeing me from those financial worries. Of course, they did not know that we had purchased a car. While they thought they were doing the right thing, they had now put us in a difficult position. School was about to start, and our oldest son had to have a uniform. We didn't even have money to purchase basic food. And it would be a month before my next paycheck would arrive. I could count on that one and all other ones thereafter because, after talking to my parents, I had called my credit union and arranged for them to send the money to a local bank in Australia bypassing my parents altogether. But what would we do for an entire month?

Fortunately for us all the neighbors along the road where we were living went out of their way to help us. One neighbor purchased our son's uniform. Another filled our gas tank, and still others insisted we come to their houses for dinner. They brought us staples and breakfast cereal. Not only did they trust us to pay them back when our money arrived, but they continued to help us in many ways throughout the entire year that we were there. We would never forget their kindness and generosity.

After the first month, Jim returned to America, but he was only there for a short time before he decided to quit his job and join us in Australia. I could already hear my parents' scorn as they commented on how I had ruined Jim's career with all for my silly ideas of traveling to some foreign country where the people may speak English but they are still foreigners! I did feel bad. But Jim seemed to be happy with his decision. Within a week of his arrival he had found a job working with some Italians from the old country. He loved his job because his co-workers thought he was a member of the Mafia, and, to keep from disappointing them, he made up stories hinting at his shady activities. Like many Australians we met, they had perceptions of America as a crime-ridden country where shootings happened daily, and people had to hide indoors. They had clearly watched too many American movies. Jim, a born storyteller, gave them such graphic descriptions of gangsters that he had them believing he was highly placed in the organization. The Italians were enthralled.

The Australian school system sorted students into two types. Students going to college went to college-oriented high schools, and those who did not plan to go in that direction went to trade high schools. I found myself in a college-oriented high school, a school without a football team, a basketball team or any other competitive sports. What a unique idea – a focus on education! I didn't have to worry about the football coach coming into my classroom pleading with me to give his star football player a passing grade even though the clod had not completed one assignment all year. Unfortunately for my Australian counterpart, he perceived the American high school as a trade school and was not happy about it at all. But he needn't have worried. My principal assigned all my regular classes to other teachers in the English department and sent the Australian to the junior high to teach remedial classes. That must have made him even less happy with his American experience. The entire time we were in Australia we would hear, "Poor Tony, he is having such a difficult time." He did like American beer but said it wasn't as good as Australian brands. His wife hated our house because it had stairs, and she was afraid her children would fall down them. Someone at the high school sold Tony a car that he used for the year and then that same person bought it back at the same price. Tony had people helping him constantly, but still he was unhappy and missed watching the Australian Rules footie games on the "telly."

We, on the other hand, loved every moment we spent in Australia even when confronted with problems that seemed beyond solution. But just as our financial fiasco was solved with the help of people who barely knew us when we first arrived, we knew we could count on other Australians to help us managed whatever other problems arose. One of the most pressing problems involved my teaching assignment. I had read about prejudice but I had never experienced it personally until then.

When I first arrived at the high school, the elderly woman principal greeted me warmly and told me she had given me light assignments so that I could take time off to visit other schools and learn about the different educational systems in Australia. However, a few months after school began, she had a heart attack and had to retire. The person who took over her position was a man who was clearly insecure. He must have found running a school a challenge because now that he was in power, he made sure that everyone knew it. I quickly found my teaching assignments had increased from a total of fifty students to one hundred and fifty. He took away my preparation periods and told me that I could not leave to visit other schools. He found excuses to send his administrative assistant to visit my classroom while class was in session so she could report back to him anything and everything she deemed a weakness in my teaching style. Since she had no background in education, she had no idea what to look for, but knowing the principal wanted negative comments, she either described some minor detail as if it were a horrendous problem, or she simply made up stories that suggested the classroom was in chaos. At least twice a day the principal would call me into his office and read the assistant's notes and then threatened me. He said he was going to write letters to the administrators in my American school to inform them of how incompetent I was.

At odd times he came into my classroom and in front of the entire class yelled. "You damn Americans do not belong here, and especially you. A woman's place is in the home." He said that his son, (who was sitting in the class at the time), could not write, and it was clearly my fault. His son was in my senior language class and was an extremely poor student. I had to wonder what the kid had been doing for the first eleven years of his education.

Fortunately, the majority of my students were hard working and intelligent and stood up for me. If they saw the principal enter the classroom, they immediately stopped whatever discussion we were having and buried their heads in their textbooks, so that our lively discussions evaporated into complete silence. Sometimes a student would raise his or her hand and make some comment about how I had enlightened him or her about a particular subject. Then, after the principal left, the atmosphere would relax, and we would continue with our discussions relevant to the topic we were studying. Despite the interruptions from the administration, I looked forward to these classes. I believe I learned as much from the students as they learned from me. Many of them had fathers who worked for mining companies or had parents who were professors at universities. They had lived in many parts of the world, and their background knowledge enriched our discussions and contributed to the students' understanding of culture and context as it was depicted in literature. Their written work was often thoughtfully planned with many creative approaches to their essays that made reading them interesting.

On the days when I had the visits from the principal I would go home highly stressed. But, still I did not let his ranting ruin my life. In fact, his off-the-wall behavior worked to my advantage. Fellow teachers came to my rescue taking my classes on days the principal was out of the building. They helped me write up the lengthy reports that I was required to complete for each student.

The principal's reputation for being an insensitive and incompetent administrator quickly spread throughout the community. One day, a doctor called and asked me to come in for an exam. I was puzzled since I was not sick. When I was finally in the examination room the doctor told me that my stress was a threat to my health, and he prescribed a two-week vacation. At first I protested that I was doing fine, but he assured me that he knew all about the new principal and that I must take the two weeks off. He asked me if my family and I had been to Tasmania and when I said no, he suggested we go there to visit friends. (We knew no one in Tasmania.) He told me that he had written a letter to the principal telling him that I was required to take two weeks off to recuperate from my illness and that I would be out of town visiting friends. I was amazed. Here was a person I have never met who had decided that while he could not solve the problem completely, he was going to make it less miserable. He was, like so many Australians we met, eager to make our stay in his country a positive one. So, on the doctor's advice, we went to Tasmania.

Our trip to the lush green island of Tasmania was pleasant contrast to the dry brown landscape of Australia proper. I remember the rugged wilderness of the west coast. If I were sent there by the doctor to "heal" then this area of Tasmania was the perfect place for that to happen. The beauty and peacefulness helped to remove all the stress that had built up from the day-to-day encounters with the principal at the high school. We rented a car and drove about the island visiting Port Arthur, a former convict settlement started in the eighteen hundreds by Great Britain who shipped its undesirable citizens there. The convicts lived under miserable conditions and were forced to build many multistoried buildings and colonial houses for the use of the men in charge. Today, there are thirty buildings that have been converted into museums and made accessible to the public. When we visited on a sunny day the area looked like a lovely place to live, so it was difficult to connect with the extremely poor conditions in which the convicts lived many years before.

Tasmania is famous for its many unique animals, like the Tasmanian devil, the fairy penguins and the platypus. We visited an animal park where we were able to see a couple of devils sleeping in an enclosure. They looked to be about the size of small dogs, but their features resembled rats. We were told that these animals have a fierce temper and huge fangs that have earned them their name. We saw only quiet creatures sleeping. We were more excited to see the platypus since it is such an unusual animal. It has webbed feet, a paddle shaped tail and a duck-like bill. They are very difficult to see in the wild, so we were happy that one was living in a pond at the park. It was a rather small animal that simply swam back and forth and probably wished it were still out in the wild.

We traveled to a beach where we had learned we could see the fairy penguins. These animals are the smallest penguins in the world, standing only one foot high. What was interesting is that these small animals had an exhausting daily routine. They waddled down to the ocean each morning, spent the day looking for food in the water and then struggled up the beach each evening just before dark. I found it difficult to watch these small creatures struggling so hard to cross the wide beach and finally crawl into their habitats in the low-lying shrubs. But signs made it clear that humans were not to interfere with the natural course of the animal routines. I suppose there were lots of people like me who were tempted to run down onto the beach and help the tiny ones up to their nests. But, of course, we watched nature take its course from the viewing deck.

One night at dusk as we were driving along a quiet road, we saw a movement on the shoulder. We stopped to look more closely and saw a wombat begin digging furiously. In less than a minute it had disappeared into the ground. How lucky we were to see such a rare sight!

All the animal encounters were wonderful antidotes for the stress I had been feeling for months. It also helped to visit all the forested wilderness areas that were so much more like home than the Australian continent that was so desert-like. When the two weeks were up we flew back to Melbourne happy and healthy. It was a good thing I felt revitalized because as soon as I returned to the high school I was summoned to the principal's office, and as I walked to his office I could already feel the stress returning.

The principal told me he didn't believe that I had been ill and that I was a typical shiftless American trying to work the system. He said he was going to report me to my school in America for taking an unauthorized vacation. That quickly elevated my stress to a much higher level. The Australian community could see what the principal was like, but my school district would only know that an administrator was complaining about me. I worried that I might lose my job when I returned to America. And when I did return home a year later I discovered that the Australian principal did write a letter, but the district administrator, who had approved the teacher exchange had received the letter, found it incomprehensible and trashed it. I was always grateful to her for making sure that letter never made it into my permanent teaching files.

On the first big school holiday Jim and I managed to put together enough money to join a bus/camping tour that drove into the center of the country. Sleeping in the Outback on the ground was an adventure. Everyone on the bus had to help unload the bus, put up tents and distribute sleeping bags. It was exciting to be in the middle of nowhere with vast expanses of land visible in every direction. After dark the sky was alive with masses of stars. The daytime heat kept the desert ground warm, which was very pleasant while lying in the tent staring up at the sky, but, at the same time, it attracted scorpions and snakes, some of the deadliest creatures in the world. Jim had a phobia about snakes and I was paranoid about spiders and scorpions. While we had netting over the front of the tent, it seemed flimsy and inadequate when all we could think of was deadly creatures finding an opening and coming into the tent. It certainly sent a tingle through our toes. I was still trying to adjust to the tarantulas that ran around on the ceiling of the house where we were living and where I had learned to sleep with a sheet over my head just in case a spider decided to jump down onto the bed, but being in a tent on the ground eyeball to eyeball with a deadly creature was even more disconcerting. I managed to suppress the need to go to the bathroom at night since it required me to climb out of the tent and try to find a bush in the dark with only a small flashlight. There was no way I was going to squat in that desert blackness where who knows what creature might want to cozy up to my rear end. And besides, if I were bitten on the behind, how would I explain that to a doctor? How embarrassing! Jim and the boys, on the other hand, could easily get out of the tent and stand somewhere without having to worry as much about the night creatures. Still, with all our worries, we managed to fall asleep and wake with no undesirable visitors inside our tent.

Morning routines required us to help pack all the equipment up to store on the bus. As we dismantled the tents we were told to be careful to look before folding the tent since there were poisonous spiders called Red Backs that lived under rocks and might find a place under a warm tent flooring. With no deadly spiders or snakes in the Pacific Northwest, I was constantly worried about our three children especially after Jim found one of them poking a snake. They had no clue that it was dangerous.

When we arrived in Alice Springs we met our first aborigines. The people we talked to were very intelligent and artistic. Their carvings, paintings and crafts were fine depictions of their cultural beliefs. So it was distressful to hear some Australians talk about the aborigines as if they were nonhuman. Most Australians live on the eastern coast. If they had never traveled into the interior of the continent, they would have no idea of what the aborigines were like. Their insensitivity was typical of people who make judgments without knowing the facts. It didn't help that the government showed a lack of sensitivity to aborigines as well. Land that belonged to these original inhabitants of Australia was often taken away and given to foreigners for development. The best example that we encountered was when we visited Ayers Rock. That we did after visiting the camels.

On our way out of Alice Springs we came to a ranch where camels were bred. We were surprised to find these animals in Australia as we, like most people, thought that camels lived in the Middle East. The owner of the ranch told us that camels had been introduced to the continent many years before because they made such good pack animals and their feet were perfect for the desert conditions in the interior of the continent. The offspring of those first camels were still living in the desert, many having gone feral. The ranch owner and his help had rounded up some of these camels and had domesticated them for local use.

When we learned that we could take a camel ride, the kids and I were quick to sign up. These camels had only one hump, so the seating was a bit dicey as we were basically sitting on the top of the hump. I rode with my youngest son since he was too small to ride alone. When we started out the camel trod along at a gentle pace with all the other camels taking people on rides. But at some point, the camel knew it was time to return to the corral, and it took off in a gallop that was so jarring I felt as if I was airborne much of the time. While my son was hanging on to the straps and apparently enjoying the fast pace, I found it impossible to grip the straps and keep myself upright. Suddenly, I was under the camel with straps wrapped around my legs keeping me from dragging on the ground. All I could think about is whether my son was okay. I couldn't see anything as the camels kicked up dust so thick it was difficult to breathe. When we reached the corral, the camel skidded to a stop, his huge padded feet churning up volumes of thick dirt that blocked my air passages making me gag. Fortunately, people came rushing over to extract me from the camel and put me upright on my feet. As I sneezed and coughed the debris out of my lungs, I looked down to see layers of grime covering my arms and legs and probably my face as well. As soon as I could speak I asked about my son, but he had ridden the camel the entire way enjoying the wild ride. You would think my husband would be concerned about whether I was okay or not, but all he could say was that the camel was going too fast so he couldn't get a good picture. The tangled straps left bruise marks up and down my legs making my walk look like those cartoon pictures of cowboys with bowed legs. I could only move at a slow pace while every muscle in both legs screamed. It took several days before I could walk normally again but what a memorable adventure. Even with the pain the ride was well worth it!

As we continued south back towards Melbourne, we stopped at Ayers Rock. This was one of the most popular tourist destinations in the country. Most visitors came to take pictures, climb to the top of the rock or walk around its base. The largest monolith in the world was more than six miles in diameter so few people made it all the way around. Most people preferred to climb to the top. The rock had no indentation or outcroppings to grip, so the authorities had installed a rope for visitors to use to pull themselves up. The result was that a continuous line of people in single file steadily climbed the rock. Anyone who lost his/her grip fell to certain death. We did not know this when we decided to make the climb. It was not until we were half way up the side of the rock that we discovered how dangerous the climb was. The rock was so smooth that even tennis shoes had no traction on the surface. The only safety "net" was the rope. We would have liked to turn around and return to the base of the rock but the long line of people behind us made that impossible. The descent had to be made using the same rope, so we had no choice but to continue up to the top, and then come down after all the climbers were up. When we finally were able to return to the base, someone pointed out the graveyard where there were stones in memory of the various individuals who had tumbled off the rock and died.

I was so relieved after we all reached the ground after finding the rock climb so dangerous. But in addition to that danger, we found out that Uluru (Ayers Rock), was a sacred place for the aborigines. All the land and the rock itself belonged to the aborigines, and they did not want people outside of their culture desecrating it. I felt awful to learn this after the fact. Why didn't someone tell us we were not supposed to climb the rock? I had to say that our ignorance could only be blamed on ourselves. The authorities should have told us, but we also should have read about Uluru before we visited.

Continuing further south we came to Coober Pedy. When we stepped off the bus all we could see for miles was barren, dry earth. We immediately came upon a sign that said, "These premises are off limits. Anyone using the water and shower facilities will be shot." With that welcome we were allowed to walk around the area where the retail stores were located. There were only a few small businesses advertising opals for sell, and, like the rest of the people on the tour bus, we quickly entered one of the shops to get out of the sun that was beating down on us. The temperature was in the hundreds in the shade. This was certainly a miserable place to live. We heard all kinds of stories of the person who arrived, found the opal of everyone's dreams, sold it for huge sums of money and moved away. Unfortunately, most of the people searching for opals were still dreaming of becoming rich.

We were told that most residents lived underground, and one family let us visit their house to see what it was like. The rooms were nicely decorated and looked like any normal house anywhere except for the walls made of rock and the lack of windows. But being underground, the temperature was comfortable and had to be many degrees below that of the outside. With a limited water supply and no pleasing landscape, the people living here had to be hardy souls. To get a sense of just how dreary the place was one need only see the movie, *Mad Max*, which was filmed here.

Jim and I wandered into one opal shop, and I asked the lady working there if she had any uncut rock with an opal vein that I could buy. I was not particularly interested in the polished opal jewelry, but I thought a chunk of rock with some opal would make a great paperweight and also be a nice souvenir. The clerk produced a piece of rock about the size of a pack of cards. It had huge streaks of red running through the center and its jagged form was aesthetically interesting. But she wanted twenty dollars. Was it worth it? Neither Jim nor I had any idea what a piece of opal was worth, or what it should look like. We decided to find the Australian friends we had met on the bus tour and get their advice. When we returned with our friends, the owner of the shop was there. We asked to look at the chunk of rock, and the clerk put it on the counter. Before our friends had a chance to even look at the rock, the owner snatched it up and told us we could not buy it. He said that the amount of opal in the rock would make over $10,000 worth of gemstones. I had to settle for another piece of rock with a tiny green streak in it. Too bad! Jim has never let me forget the rock that we could have taken home worth so much money. Of course, having seen the sign at the entrance to Coober Pedy about being shot for using the facilities, I am sure had I been able to purchase the red opal rock and even gotten on the bus with it, that the owner would have come after me and made me return it. I don't know if he owned a gun, but chances are pretty high that he did since he probably had more than one valuable piece of opal in his shop. We left the barren hills of Coober Pedy and headed south to Melbourne and back to our temporary home just in time to return to teaching.

On another school holiday, we drove up the eastern coast of Australia camping out in pup tents. It was the rainy season although the temperature was warm. We were living out of our car so much of the time that we were wet and soggy, but we didn't mind. We had hoped to find an affordable way to visit the Great Barrier Reef. After some inquiries we found a boat that was taking scuba divers out on a day trip to the Reef. Although the water was choppy, and the trip was a very rough ride, we simply were too excited about seeing the Reef to care. After a couple of hours, the boat stopped in a channel. On either side were coral formations. We watched as the scuba divers donned their equipment and jumped overboard. The water was so clear that we could see them even after they had gone down well below the surface. The boat owners gave us snorkeling gear and told us to stay close to the boat. As soon as we were in the ocean with our facemasks immersed, we could see all kinds of marine life: coral waving in the water as if being blown by a strong wind and fish of every color, shape and size. It was like swimming inside an aquarium. It was all so exciting, but there was one experience that was actually "heart stopping" for me. A gigantic clamshell lay on the edge of the coral with its mouth wide open revealing a gorgeous velvety blue interior. I decided to swim down for a closer look and when my foot was inside the opening, the shell snapped shut capturing me. I tried not to panic but not expecting this to happen and feeling as if I had little air left in my lungs, my first reaction was to try to pull my foot loose. As my lungs lost air, I became even more frantic. Luckily, a scuba diver came over and motioned for me to be as still as possible, and once I did, the clamshell opened its jaws and I quickly swam to the surface gasping for air. What a frightening experience! Naturally, after my panic attack I worried about the three children and what they were doing. They were all good swimmers and none of them were having any problems at all. Jim was also a strong swimmer and was watching the kids as he looked about. My experience left me exhausted, and I decided to clamor back into the boat and watch the rest of the family enjoying themselves.

After we returned to the mainland, we excitedly discussed our incredible experience. We wanted to see more of the Reef, so Jim and I did some calculating and shifted this priority and that and then decided we could go out once more to the Reef. We had only one day left before we had to head south and back to the place where we were living. We made some more inquiries and finally settled on the only viable way to visit the Reef a second time. We wanted to see Heron Island because it had a research station and was not as commercial as many of the coral islands further north.

We only had a day to find a means of going out to Heron Island, so we drove to a small airport nearby and asked about making a one-day trip. The rainy season meant that few planes were flying. But one pilot told us that if we showed up really early the next morning, he would let us go with him on his daily reconnaissance flight to check the conditions on the Reef. He seemed to have found our three children's enthusiasm so great he wanted to give them one last opportunity to see nature's coral wonderland.

The next morning we showed up a couple hours early. After we got settled in the plane, he took off circling the coastline and then heading out to sea. The aerial view of the Reef was an amazing sight, and we were all the more eager to return to the airport and find someone to take us out for the day. When we returned, the pilot introduced us to a helicopter pilot who said he would take us out to Heron Island the next day and then come back in the evening to return us to the mainland. He also said he would only charge us for the cost of two adults and the children could go for free.

We wanted to go so badly but spending another day where we were would make our drive back to the home outside Melbourne a long trip. We would have no time to stop and camp. We would have to drive all day and perhaps part of the evening to return in time for me to go back to work on time. We decided we had to do it. It was a lifetime experience.

The next morning we drove to the airport in heavy fog. We were all silent thinking that our chance to see the Reef that day was not likely to happen. We tried to remain optimistic, but we could barely see cars in front of us, so flying seemed even less likely. When we arrived at the airport there was a helicopter waiting for us. The pilot appeared from the office and said that normally he didn't like to fly in such fog, but he was going to try as reports indicated that the weather at Heron Island was sunny. We boarded the plane, and I remember thinking how scary it was to be suspended in a heavy gray mist so that it didn't seem as if we were moving forward but were staying in one spot in the air. But happily, after about thirty minutes we broke through the fog and could finally see the water below us. With such a huge expanse of ocean I still had the sensation of hanging in space. Finally about an hour later we saw a small island below us.

When we landed the pilot gave us detailed instructions to be back at the landing pad at a specific time that evening, and the next thing we knew, he had flown away. A lady who owned a scuba diving company told us that she had held up her boat so that we could come aboard. We told her we were not scuba divers. She said that we could snorkel while the other people on board were diving, but we had to hurry since the trip was behind schedule. We simply waded out and climbed the ladder on the back of the boat and immediately we were off. The boat headed out through a channel between coral formations and suddenly the calm water had turned to choppy waves that made the boat bounce about in many directions, and we had to hold onto the railings to keep from falling overboard. This didn't seem to bother any of the scuba divers who began attaching their gear. The boat stopped, and the scuba divers jumped overboard. It was amazing to look down and see the divers exploring in the crystal clear water. Jim, the kids and I stripped down to our bathing suits and crawled down the ladder. The water was a bit chilly, but any discomfort we felt at first was quickly forgotten as soon as we entered the sea. Once we immersed our facemasks we could see a colorful array of coral and fish. Like our previous experience, we felt as if we were in another aquarium.

Jim and the kids had a great time, but I found the choppy water very hard to handle. I kept choking and coughing, and my weak swimming skills quickly made me tired. Then, while treading water and trying to get my breath, Jim yelled that he had seen a shark. His excitement made me flail my arms, and I gulped too much water. Panic set in. Where were the kids? All I could think of was getting them back in the boat to safety.

The operator of the boat must have seen the shark as well, for he began yelling and gesturing to us. I struggled against waves that began lifting me up and then dropping me into troughs where water would come crashing over me. The motion of the sea kept pushing me away from the boat and toward a reef with its razor sharp coral. And then, just when I felt so exhausted I could not swim any more, I saw a buoy that the operator had thrown into the water. I grasped it and held on while he reeled me in like some huge fish. As I was being towed back to the boat I could see Jim and the kids already on deck yelling and waving at me. Finally, I crawled up the ladder and lay on the wood flooring completely spent. Jim was still talking about his close encounter with the shark. He went in to elaborate detail and then had to repeat his description for the scuba divers who had missed the excitement and were now clamoring into the boat for our return through the channel into the peaceful waters inside the reef. It was such a memorable event and for years after our return from Australia, Jim loved telling about his shark encounter.

Once we had returned to the mainland, we had to drive most of the night so that I could be at school the next day. The rest of the school year went very quickly, and soon we had to say goodbye to our many new friends. The Australian summer vacation started at the end of December, so when Jim and I and the children returned home, we found the adjustment to winter a bit of a shock. But I couldn't think about the weather as the second semester of school was about to begin, and I had to be ready to teach.

We learned a lot from our year in Australia. The kids had learned to adjust to a different culture and lifestyle. They had to rethink how people lived in a desert climate as opposed to the rainy Northwest in America. They discovered that most children had to wear uniforms to school that not only included slacks and sweaters but also blazers, hats and gloves. The formality of the school uniforms fascinated our children, who were used to the more casual styles in America. The children came home with a greater view of the world, particularly Southeast Asia and had become comfortable with traveling outside the U.S. so that in later life none of them felt the anxiety I had when I first left America.

Jim found Australia to be just as interesting as he had thought when he first talked about going there. He loved working with the first generation Italians and also found the travel experience opened up new worlds to him. He liked it so much that years later he wanted to return to visit friends we had made on that epic journey into the center. Over the years we have stayed connected to them. They came to America, and we returned to visit them in Australia.

I also learned a lot from our year in Australia. I discovered that living and working in a foreign country was a much different experience from visiting on a tour. I had to cope with prejudice and learn to adjust to a completely different teaching system then what I was used to at home. But most importantly, I learned that Australians are, with minor exceptions, kind, caring and helpful. Moving to a different culture presented us with many problems, but my family and I found the effort to solve them challenging and rewarding. On my return to America, I felt renewed, and the routine I had disliked so much now seemed to be fine, at least for the time being.

Dare To Do It!

Kangaroos can only be found in the Outback, so many Australians have only seen them in zoos.

A reproduction of a 19th century town in the Outback.

The main road into the center of Australia.

The path on the top of Ayers Rock.

Lots of dangerous creatures live in Australia.

Nancy Rubesch

CHINA

When my family and I returned to the United States from Australia, Jim managed to secure his old job back, and I returned to teaching at the high school. Although every day was predictable, I wasn't bored. I was actually happy. I was so engrossed in Jim's sports and the children's multitude of activities that I simple enjoyed being a mom.

Four months after our return in December, a colleague handed me a flyer advertising an opportunity to go to China. I had become fascinated with Chinese calligraphy and had taken several beginning language classes, so a trip to China would be perfect, but having just returned from Australia and heavily in debt, there was no way I could justify going. But it was 1980 and China had just opened up after the Cultural Revolution. This had to be an historic time to visit.

I tried to forget the article describing the trip that was scheduled for that coming summer. The idea gnawed at my mind until I finally decided to find out more details. I knew I was just making myself miserable since my going was completely hopeless. I called the professor who was leading the group tour to China. He told me that a wealthy businessman associated with Duke University was sponsoring the trip and had agreed to bring a hundred Americans to China on a cultural exchange. Unfortunately, it was now May, and the Chinese government red tape had taken so long to process that now that the exchange was approved, it was too late to find that many participants. When I explained my interest but lack of funds, the professor said he would talk with the businessman and see if anything could be done to help me.

A couple of days later, the professor called me back. He said that the businessman, who was supposedly friends with Deng Xiaoping, the leader of China at the time, was willing to pay for my trip. He was already sponsoring another participant. From what the professor said, I came to the conclusion that the businessman wanted to "save face." He had apparently made a promise to deliver a big group of Americans, and only a handful of participants had applied to go. The fact that he was willing to pay for my trip left me speechless. In complete silence I listened as the professor explained what I needed to do: obtain a visa and make sure my passport was up-to-date. He said he would send me all the material I needed including the flight information and where to meet the rest of the group.

I rushed about making all the arrangements necessary for the trip to China. When I told Jim that I wanted to go he was less than enthusiastic, but understanding. He would be playing softball all summer, and the children loved to watch him. He, in turn, loved going to their sports games. They would be doing what they had planned to do for the summer anyway except that I would not be there. That was okay with the children, as they knew that Jim would feed them fast food, whereas if I were home I would make them eat more healthy fare. During the day when Jim was at work the children would be attending summer workshops that would keep them busy.

At the end of the school year I packed my bag and headed to the airport where I met the professor and his wife. There were two other participants with them, a young woman and her boyfriend, both Seattle residents. The couple was so delightful that, despite the fact that I was twenty years older, the three of us hit it off from the start and became close friends. The young woman and I decided to be roommates, and enjoyed each other's company so much that we continued to keep in contact for years later.

When we arrived in China, an escort took us to a residential hotel where we would spend the summer. Once there we met the rest of the group, an interesting mix of young and old, students, workers, and artists. I wondered how the trip had been advertised given the assortment of people that composed the group. As it turned out there were only twenty of us. Some of the participants were friendly, but others were rather distant. Their reasons for going to China were unclear. I assumed they were all interested in the history of China and its current political state, but at least one older lady had packed all her favorite clothing and as soon as we were settled at the university where we would study, had sent the clothing off to a tailor to have the styles duplicated in different materials. She seemed uninterested in studying Chinese and must have had an unpleasant personality because, at one point, the professor and his wife asked me to room with her, as her assigned roommate did not like her. Of course, by then my Seattle roommate and I were soul mates, and we refused to split up. The final solution was to provide the lady with her own private room even though it was inconvenient for the Chinese authorities. Most of the other participants did not leave a lasting impression on my mind. I only remember some of them talking about how careful they had to be because they thought that taking one step away from the established routine would have dire consequences. Unlike their paranoia, I had no such concerns.

The very first day in Hofei I went out for a walk by myself and got lost. I had no phrase book, no phone, no address and no map. I didn't even know the name of the hotel. I didn't think I had walked that far, but suddenly I found myself at a huge intersection, and I could see nothing that looked familiar. I stood there on the sidewalk while a large crowd began to gather. I looked about and saw hundreds of curious faces looking at me. Some were whispering to each other while others just stood with mouths gaping. With blue eyes and blond hair I was clearly a bit of a standout! In any case, my hopes that someone would step forward who spoke English did not happen. What could I do?

In the middle of the intersection was a tiny round booth sitting on a cement podium high enough off the ground for the traffic cop standing in the booth to be seen by the vehicles all converging at the center. I walked out into the intersection and when I reached the booth, I yelled up to the policeman asking for help, and I remember he looked at me with great distress. I had just ruined his day. He had to get the traffic moving, and my presence had stopped the flow in all directions. I stood there as the crowd press in on me. Everyone was friendly, but clearly those in the back were pushing forward. I was basically hugging the podium while the policeman was talking on his phone, obviously, asking for help. It seemed like an incredibly long time to wait to be rescued because I began to feel like I was suffocating. It was a very hot day and then with all these people breathing so close to my face, I felt as if I might pass out. Finally, through the crowd came a man, who spoke English. He asked me to follow him. He led me back to the hotel where a hotel employee handed me a piece of paper written in Chinese characters. Translated, it said, "I am lost, please take me to the Central Hotel in Hofei."

After that first day of disastrous adventure, I decided it would be best to go with my roommate, who had a great sense of direction and could be counted on to get us back to the hotel. One morning before the summer session started she and I set out in the early morning hours to explore. We encountered a group of elderly men and women doing tai chi exercises. I stared in astonishment when I saw a gray haired lady standing next to a lamppost with one leg stretched completely vertical. I watched a man doing several poses where he stood for several minutes on one leg completely motionless with one leg planted against the other and his arms overhead, his hands forming a pray pose. I was only half the age of either one of them, and I could not do those same stretches. I, who regularly practiced yoga, could not make my body perform in that manner, nor did I have the balance to stand so quietly for such a long period of time. I marveled at the discipline of these elderly Chinese and wondered how many Americans could do the same.

Dare To Do It!

The city where we would spend the summer studying the Chinese language and culture was small compared to other cities in China, and yet it had a million and one-half inhabitants. At that time local authorities were just beginning to clean up the ravages of the Cultural Revolution. At the university where we would attend classes, most of the buildings had shattered windows or empty holes with the glass that should have been there scattered on the ground below. Every building was in complete disrepair save the ground floor of one unit where we Americans would attend classes. Later when we, as a group, traveled we saw the same destructive effect of the Cultural Revolution as well. During that time period, Mao Zedong had encouraged young people to travel throughout the country denouncing and destroying anything that was bourgeois, and that included educational institutions.

The city of Hofei, where we studied, was the capital of the poorest province in China and had no tourist infrastructure. The city was really off the beaten path so it seemed strange to me that we foreigners would be brought here to study. Perhaps the central government chose Hofei for the very reason that, as a backwater, if we foreigners caused any problems, they would be able to contain them without the fuss that might occur in Beijing or Shanghai where there were international news agencies. Since the country was just beginning to reestablish ties with other countries, they, more than likely, would not want to broadcast negative news to the world particularly if it involved foreigners.

The local authorities assigned a "tongzhi," a comrade, to each American. These Chinese students were expected to report our daily activities and make sure we didn't wander alone about the city. We asked for maps but only received them months after we had begun classes. But, even without maps, my roommate and I were not going to sit around in the hotel like some of the other group participants. We would take off to explore a different part of the city each day as soon as the Chinese comrades had gone home. As a result, we were not the best students in the classes, but what we learned on the streets was as valuable as what was being taught in the classroom

When my roommate's boyfriend came with us, we would all meet his tongzhi at some local restaurant. When we arrived, we had to quickly duck into the doorway and rush upstairs to the second floor where we could talk without being seen by people passing on the street. This was important since it was against the law for groups to gather in public. Usually, the tongzhi brought many of his friends so that the group could be quite large and lively as we compared the differences between America and Chinese societies. At that time, foreign literature, such as newspapers and magazines were unavailable, so the students were eager to talk with us about the outside world, a world that had been closed off to them for all of their lives.

Some of the Chinese students complained about being unable to purchase high quality products, such as small appliances, as these were only sold in special stores reserved for Chinese dignitaries and their families. These stores also sold souvenirs to tourists. To buy a product at the special store one had to have 'funny money,' a special currency issued to foreigners and available to the dignitaries. The few tourists who came to China at this time were herded about to sightseeing spots and then to the special stores where they could acquire the souvenirs they might wish to take home.

Our group was only allowed the funny money, but it didn't take long before we were complaining because we had run out of toothpaste or shampoo, and these products were only sold in ordinary stores using the official currency of China, the Renminbi. The tongzhi's friends wanted to exchange Renminbi for funny money, and that was fine with us since we could purchase our toiletries in the local shops and the Chinese students could use the funny money at the specialty stores. If they tried to purchase something there, the sales people would assume they were related to some high-powered dignitary and would not question them. (Today, China uses only the Renminbi and the funny money has disappeared.)

Our meals often consisted of stir-fried rice and vegetables and some times a small portion of pork. After a couple of months on a minimalist diet, I was probably healthier than at home, but I began craving sugar. I found a shop where I could purchase a couple of cookies, and even though the sugar content was low, the pleasure of tasting just a tiny bit of sugar was supremely satisfying. Of course, I told the other Americans, and soon we were all flocking to the bakery. A couple of days later, the tour leader called us together to explain that we were not allowed to purchase any product that consisted of flour, sugar or butter. All of these were in short supply, and the government had issued rationing coupons to residents. The salespeople had sold us the cookies because they could see we didn't understand the situation, but they also reported the problem to their supervisors. The tour leader arranged for each of us to receive a few coupons, but when I discovered my purchases were depriving some hard working Chinese person of his or her quota, I decided to forego the cookies. At the end of summer when I was in Shanghai I did find White Rabbit candy, a sugary concoction I would never eat at home but which I gobbled down at once. I was surprised to find I had such a deep dependency on sugar.

That summer I learned what it was like to live in a country totally controlled by the central government. I remember students saying that they did not dare to date in college because once they graduated they could be sent anywhere in the country to work whatever job the government decreed. Even at that time there were many married people who lived far apart because of their assignments, and they only saw each other once a year during the one vacation allotted to them. If we ran into some Chinese friends from the restaurant, they would greet us but continue walking, afraid to stop should a policeman see us conversing. While the government did not allow group gatherings of Chinese, a group gathering that included foreigners would be even worse. It was clear that the authorities in Hofei were as paranoid as some of the participants in our group. This cultural exchange was the first of its kind in the city and probably one of the very few anywhere in the entire country, so the local authorities wanted to be sure everything went smoothly, else they would have to answer to the central government in Beijing. That would not be a positive thing! Although I tried to keep an open mind about the Chinese society, I could not help but compare Chinese lives to American ones, and I realized how grateful I was to live in America where we had so much freedom.

That summer I also learned how to be independent in an "alien" environment. In Europe it was easy to recognize businesses and even sound out some foreign words. But in Hofei, I could not read the Chinese characters and my speaking ability was limited to saying simple phrases like, "hello" or "goodbye." When I walked down the street of the city I had no idea what business I was passing. Looking in the window and seeing the interior was not always a clue. The business might be a bank, or it might be a post office. I might see someone sitting in a chair and assume it was a barbershop when if fact it could be a dentist office. Restaurants were easy enough to recognize, but I had no clue as to the type of food being served. There were no fast food shops. Stores selling clothing were identifiable because of the displays in the windows, but if I went inside looking for the items I had seen, they simply didn't exist. Most of the citizens of Hofei had never seen foreigners before. In 1980, the only media available in the country were Chinese news agency broadsides attached to walls in the central area of the city and a couple of news journals. Many people were illiterate. At the post office there would be people sitting on the steps leading into the building. They held signs offering to write letters or fill out forms for anyone who needed the service. At the banks, instead of a signature, when I exchanged a money order for cash, I had to "sign" with my thumbprint. Calculations were done with an abacus. The daily activities I would take for granted at home were always an adventure here in China. I loved every minute of it.

When my roommate and I would head out after classes in the afternoon to explore the city, she never walked beside me, but would hurry over to the opposite side of the street where her Japanese-American features made it possible for her to blend in, especially when she wore Chinese clothing she had purchased since coming to the city. I bought Chinese clothing too but my blond hair made me stand out and no matter where I went, curious locals would begin to follow me. Soon more people would join in and crowds would form. If we went into a store to purchase something, the crowds would follow and gather about watching us. If we looked at them, they would smile and we would smile back. It would have been nice to communicate with them especially when I purchased a pair of plastic sandals that were opaque white. Apparently, each size sandal was a different color and gender. As usual the Chinese would be whispering among themselves, probably remarking about what large feet I had and wondering why I had purchased men's shoes.

Our daily routine consisted of attending lectures, studying the language, doing homework and talking with our ever-present comrades. The comrades, who Velcroed themselves to us like flies caught on sticky paper, were studying the English language. Their jobs were to watch us closely, even to accompany us to the bathroom. While they were with us throughout the school day, we were at least free of them in the evenings when we were expected to do our homework. We always had more than it seemed possible to complete. Were the authorities trying to keep us so busy we would not have time to wander about the city? In any case the expectations of the Chinese teachers were difficult for me to meet. I would practice writing Chinese characters over and over again and finally complete what I thought were fine looking examples. But I dreaded going to writing class the next day because the teacher always chose my examples to show the class how poorly I had done. She talked about how each stroke had to be rendered just so, not too long and not too short. She explained how the placement of the strokes had to be in "harmony." My work was clearly lacking in harmony. The teacher would stand in front of the class holding up my homework and drawing bright red slashes through each character while her facial expression clearly register disapproval. Her strident voice is still imprinted on my memory.

Although I was now in another daily routine, it was far from dull. But one morning I suddenly found myself exhausted and could not get out of bed. All I wanted to do was sleep. Naturally the professor, leading the group, was worried that I was sick, so he and his wife arranged for me to go to the local hospital. Outside the hospital, people were lying on blankets on the hard ground. Some looked as if they had been there for days. Apparently they had, the professor told us after he spoke to several of the people. (He was Chinese-American and spoke Mandarin fluently.)

If patients were lucky enough to get inside they were taken into an auditorium-sized room where rows of desks were arranged. People were directed to different desks and then, right in the middle of the room, were told to take off their clothes so they could be examined. Clearly, this would not do for the foreigner. I was taken into a private room. I didn't have to undress and after the doctor checked my vital signs, stuck a needle into my arm and attached an IV solution. While I was lying there, I looked up from the bed to see a window filled with faces pressed against the pane. I learned something new that day. Privacy is a luxury we Americans take for granted. For people in China there was no privacy even for medical exams. The professor talked with the doctor for a long time, but I did not understand what they were saying since they spoke in Chinese. The end result was that after I had been plumped up with the IV solution, I was taken back to the hotel and told to rest. I was diagnosed with dehydration.

Worried that if one foreigner was dehydrated the rest of the group would be as well, authorities decided they needed to provide treatment to all the foreigners. The prescription was simple: watermelons. That very next morning, men arrived filling our bathtubs with ten or more large watermelons. After the delivery, we ran around to each room to see how many watermelons had been left. There must have been at least five watermelons per person! We all decided that after eating some of the fruit we would give the rest to the hotel staff. The group leader and his wife were relieved that I was okay but delighted to have had the experience of going to the hospital to see how the Chinese handled patients seeking health care.

In addition to attending the Chinese program in Hofei, the authorities arranged to take our group on field trips to visit historic sites such as the Forbidden City and the Great Wall. I was so excited to finally see the fabled city described in Pearl Buck's novels that I completely ignored the descriptions in her stories and visualized a marvelous fairy tale-like structure worthy of royalty. So when we walked under the entrance gate with the huge portrait of Mao Zedong plastered to the outside wall forever staring out across Tian'anmen Square, I was extremely disappointed. The buildings were all low-lying structures separated by immense areas of cement. There were a few cauldrons so huge a person could easily climb inside and disappear from view. In front of the buildings were pairs of lions, traditionally serving to guard the imperial palace and protect the emperor. A few buildings had open doorways where we could look into dark and dreary interiors where a few artifacts had been placed for visitor viewing. I found the complex organization within the royal residence difficult to completely understand, and I decided that once I was back in Seattle I would enroll in a class to gain a more in-depth idea of the life of emperors and the various dynasties they ruled.

Another trip took us an hour north of Beijing to see the Great Wall. The one and only section open at that time had been restored by adding new bricks to the old, filling in gaps that would otherwise make climbing impossible. Once we had hiked up the many steps to the watch towers we had panoramic views of the countryside that was particularly dramatic embellished as it were by the ancient Wall as it snaked over the steep hillsides, disappeared behind cliffs and reappeared far in the distance. At the end of the tourist section the Wall was still in its original state of disrepair, a crumbling pile of rocks that resembled a wall only because we were told that was what it was. If it had been in some other location we would have probably thought the remains were simply a part of some ancient house instead of part of one of the most famous structures on earth. With huge gaps between the unrestored sections, it was clearly not safe for tourists. At the time of our visit, there were few tourist facilities, just a parking area for vehicles. To get to the base of the Wall we had to hike up an exceptionally steep hill. It was clearly challenging for average tourists, but we were told that a cable car would be installed in the next year to accommodate the anticipated arrival of more tourists.

On still another trip we were taken to Huangshan, the Yellow Mountains, a range of seventy peaks all towering some three thousand feet into the air. The craggy peaks were often shrouded in mists and adorned with twisted pines whose roots clung to the sheer rock in impossible ways. Poets and artists had gone there for thousands of years to contemplate nature, and their poems and paintings had made Huangshan famous.

In order to reach the top of the mountains these poets and artists had to climb, as we did, for two days, up vertical stairs, so steep that in order to keep their balance they had to do as I did, hold onto the steps directly in front of me. There were no hand railings and the hand-hewn steps were so ancient and worn that trying to step up to the next one took all of my energy. Halfway to the top, we Americans were told to stop at a large building clinging to the sides of a rocky pinnacle. It was here we would spend the night since the Chinese believed that we foreigners were not in good enough physical shape to finish the climb that day. The next morning we continued our trek. I remember looking up and seeing those stairs going straight up into the clouds with no breaks, and I thought of the popular Led Zeppelin song, "Stairway to Heaven." At this point I was no longer stepping up from one stone to another. Instead I had to crawl. The risers had so much height, one to the next, that I had to pull myself up, scoot my butt onto the stair, pull my legs up and finally get on all fours, and grab hold of the step directly in front of my nose to keep from losing my balance. I repeated this process over and over for several hours.

Because the mountains rose so sharply from the valley floor to such heights, the climate at the base could be dramatically different from that at the top. So, as I crept ever so slowly up the vertical stairs, I shouldn't have been surprised when it began raining. It had been so sunny I had only a light jacket to put on over my tee shirt. It wasn't long before the wind picked up. I remember shivering and my fingers were cold so that trying to hold on to the stone steps was difficult. What made matters worse was that with the rain, the stones were now slippery and often my grip would not hold. Trying to stand on the uneven steps was also difficult. Sometimes my shoes would grip and other times I felt like I was on a piece of ice. While I am not normally afraid of heights, I was definitely in panic mode. I could feel my body go rigid even as I tried to talk myself into relaxing. I couldn't move. Fortunately, a young Chinese laborer came up from below me, and in one smooth movement, took hold of my arm and pulled me up the remaining steps. At the top as I sat trying to regain my composure, the laborer had disappeared before I could even thank him.

Before we had begun our arduous climb, we saw Chinese laborers climbing swiftly up the stairs in front of us and disappearing from view. They carried huge slabs of stone tied to poles that were perched on their shoulders. They moved so quickly it was as if they had no burden at all, yet it was easy to see that the stone slabs were real and extremely heavy. How did those skinny malnourished-looking men manage to hike up those stairs at such a quick pace that I could not keep up, and all I had to carry was a small daypack with a bottle of water? The building at the midway point and the others at the top of the mountain were all large structures that would have had to be built by men such as the ones we saw all carrying the materials up to the top. I couldn't help but think of all the manpower it must have taken to complete this daunting task.

I remember meeting up with the group at the top of the mountain, and when the weather cleared, we descended the stairs much as we had gone up them. It was just as difficult in spots to go down, as it was to go up. When we arrived at the base of the mountains, we congratulated ourselves on a successful trek to the top. A few of the group participants, including the professor and his wife, had chosen not to do the climb, so they met us at the bottom where we gathered together, some of us bragging while the others happy they had not attempted the demanding hike up the ancient staircase.

After the Chinese language program was completed, I had a couple of weeks of summer left before having to be back at school. Because travel, accommodations and food were inexpensive I decided to join my roommate and her boyfriend to travel across China to Xian to see the terracotta warriors archeological site. At that time visitors were allowed to view the one pit that had been unearthed. As soon as the ancient site had been discovered the authorities built a roof overhead, but there were no other facilities and few visitors. Of course there would not have been many foreign visitors since only a handful of college professors and their groups had been allowed into the country. Every foreigner was required to travel with a Chinese guide, so we arranged to hire one of the Chinese students, who had participated in the summer program. As it turned out, the student was my roommate's boyfriend's tongzhi. He accompanied us to Xian but then had to leave to return to his family. The three of us, my roommate, her boyfriend and I were on our own. It was clear that we were not supposed to be traveling by ourselves, and it was easy to see the anxiety on the faces of local authorities, who didn't know what to do with us. They would quickly process our tickets and urge us to get on the train, and thus, out of their hair. They didn't want to be involved with foreigners and risk getting into trouble.

Traveling on our own with our limited language skills was a remarkable experience because we had to find ways to purchase train tickets, no small feat when an orderly line before a ticketing window would immediately erupt into chaos as soon as a window opened. The lines disappeared as everyone shoved each other this way and that trying to reach the ticketing agent. We managed to push our way to the ticket window but purchasing the actual tickets took some doing. The agent tried to ignore us and deal with all the people shouting and shoving their arms around us. Eventually, the agent, wanting to get rid of us, sold us our tickets, and then pushing and shoving, we made our way out of the station and onto the boarding platform.

We boarded the train heading for Shanghai, and spent a day and night riding across the country. At that time there were four classes for riding the train: hard and soft seats, hard and soft sleepers. The wealthy Chinese, such as the businessmen, and tourist groups rode in the soft seat/sleepers. We chose the cheaper car with its row upon row of tiered bunks. Although they were called "hard" sleepers, the bunks were padded and actually quite comfortable for sleeping.

With one set of bunks facing another, there was no privacy. Those people who had the top bunks had no room to sit up, so people with the bottom bunks were expected to share during the day. That was just fine with us because we had a chance to talk with ordinary Chinese heading home on vacations. With our dictionaries open, we were able to communicate with them and had a great time sharing information about our families.

Shanghai has been an international port since the end of the Opium Wars in the eighteen hundreds, so the city was well developed as an urban center when we arrived. Tall buildings lined the Huangpu River on one side, but the other side, called Pudong, was still filled with low lying houses and old buildings. This was the first time we encountered masses of people walking about in the streets and heavy traffic volume. In Beijing the city was spread out so that we rarely encountered any crowds and a majority of people rode bicycles. But here in Shanghai there were massive numbers of vehicles and the volume of people walking about was astonishing. There were so many people that sidewalks were packed and groups of people simply walked in the street dodging traffic. I had been to New York City and saw the crowds of people there, but that did not compare at all to the number of people I saw here.

One day while walking around, the clouds hovered overhead and we heard thunder. People started running into buildings. We noticed everyone scurrying about but didn't think too much more about it. Suddenly, a torrential downpour came down. It was as if someone were dumping buckets of water on us. This was not the Northwest United States drizzle, nor was it like the windy rain that fell when we were in the Huangshan. This was so heavy I could hardly breathe. No wonder everyone had run for cover. In an instant we were drenched as if we had been swimming in a river. We managed to press ourselves under an overhang and some ten minutes later the flood from the sky had stopped. The entire experience was frightening. It certainly was nothing I had ever encountered at home.

We spent a week in Shanghai looking for its historic past. From the 1840s through the 1940s the center of the city was divided into concessions run by different countries: Russia, America, Britain, France and German. This was where the expatriates lived. During the early 1940s the city became famous for its extravagant lifestyle of drinking and gambling. One of the symbols of this era, that can still be seen today, was the Peace Hotel, once the most luxurious hotel in Asia. But the partying came to an end when the Japanese invaded. Walking around the city, we saw remnants of each country's former occupation.

On the plane flying home I remember thinking of how generous that businessman from Duke University had been to fund my summer adventure. As soon as I arrived home I wrote a letter thanking him for making the trip a reality. I went on to describe how inspired I was by all the experiences I had encountered and that I planned to further my studies of the Chinese language and its culture. I also sent a letter to the professor and his wife thanking them for their guidance throughout our stay. I continued to stay in contact with my former roommate and her boyfriend, and we have had many wonderful times reminiscing about our first trip to China.

Over the years I have been able to return to China many times and each year I have witnessed dramatic changes throughout the country. Each time I visit I realize that no matter how much I think I know about this ancient culture, I always need to learn more. Within a few years the country had changed so much that there were places I no longer recognized. For example, the skyline of Beijing is now filled with massive numbers of skyscrapers. When I had first visited, there was only one high rise, the Beijing Hotel, and it was only four stories. The city has expanded so greatly that a subway system is the only efficient way to get about, whereas, on my first visit and even my second in the later part of the 1980s, I could find my way on a bicycle with all the other inhabitants of the city. Today, cars rule the road, and riding a bicycle would be extremely dangerous, and like all modern cities, the traffic is so heavy it barely moves in the downtown core.

Shanghai has also developed dramatically. Not only has the city expanded vertically, but it has moved across the river to the east, so that the Pudong area that had once been low lying modest houses was now completed occupied by skyscrapers. In fact, it is one of the most popular spots for tourists, who are taken to the Oriental Pearl Tower, where they can look out at the city from high above and even walk on a glass floor looking down on the traffic, the river and the mass of people flowing like ants in one direction or another.

The modernization of China has brought many problems. Every day in the newspapers I read articles about this problem or that. When Jim and I recently visited Beijing we encountered pollution so thick we could not see a few feet in front of us. The stagnant air was so dense we felt as if we were strangling each time we took a breath. We quickly found a pharmacy to purchase masks, which we wore for the rest of our time in the city. The masks made breathing difficult, but we hoped they would help filter out the bad air. Each night after walking about the city, we would take off our masks to find them discolored with flecks of black matter along with gray stains. With so much pollution we were surprised at the number of Chinese who didn't wear masks or even have them on their children.

Dare To Do It!

We also found the cities of Beijing and Shanghai crowded to overflowing. We had never seen so many people. Tian'anmen Square, one of the largest city squares in the world, is known as the place where Mao Zedong announced the beginning of the People's Republic of China, and in more recent times, the 1989 pro-democracy demonstrations that killed so many students. When I saw it the first time, it was a huge empty square with a few people here and there, but on our recent visit Jim and I found the square cordoned off and mobs of people pushing and shoving to enter the one narrow entrance that was guarded by soldiers. Once inside, the masses of people were too great for us to negotiate in any direction. The crowds were so thick we could hardly move and we finally maneuvered our way to the side and then out the exit at the far end of the square.

When we went to the Forbidden City or any other tourist sights, we encountered long lines of Chinese waiting to enter. Just walking on the streets was like walking in a crowd after a ball game in America where everyone is trying to leave at the same time. At times we found ourselves walking in the street just to proceed. But that was not safe since the vehicular traffic made no effort to slow down to avoid hitting pedestrians.

There were traffic jams at most intersections near tourist sites as bus after bus stopped in the middle of the street to disgorge groups of Chinese tourists. Many of these groups consisted of elderly folk who stopped and gaped at the world outside the bus and seemed oblivious to everyone else. One bus might not have been so bad, but we counted fifteen double-parked next to each other taking up all lanes of the street. It was a chaotic mess. Still, I could remember my first visit when citizens were not allowed to travel for pleasure. Now these rural folk were finally seeing their own country. In fact, when we were in China last year, we saw few foreigners on the streets, but it looked as if the entire Chinese population was on the move.

On our recent visit to the Great Wall we found a Disney atmosphere so different from my first view of this magnificent structure. There are now two places where visitors could access the Wall. In both places one had to walk through an "ancient" village before arriving at a cable car that hauled one to the top of the steep hillside where the actual Wall is located. While each village appears weathered and worn with buildings from a dynastic era, in fact, the village is brand new. What the tourists do not know and probably don't care is that the original village was razed and the villagers relocated to another place miles away. The "ancient" village is owned by the government, is run by Chinese paid to dress in ancient costumes and to sell as many souvenirs as possible. The authorities recognize the appeal of old and ancient structures, so they have built them just for the tourists. And the tourists love the atmosphere and perhaps enjoy exploring the shops in the village as much if not more than clamoring about on the actual Wall.

One of the areas accessible to the Wall now has an entertainment park ride that consists of a cement luge track on which carts on wheels zip down the hillside at ungodly rates of speed. If the view of the Wall were not exciting enough, the carney ride would get the thrill seekers pumped. Of course, for most visitors a ride back down on the cable car is enough of an adrenaline rush as the car sways back and forth and invariably stops at a point where they can take a moment to think about that recent news article describing a high rise that suddenly collapsed due to shoddy construction and wonder about that cable, the tiny one keeping the car from suddenly breaking loose and plunging onto the rocks and debris far below. Happily everyone usually makes it safely to the bottom of the mountain, to buy souvenirs and climb on board their respective buses to head off to another important site.

Even the artistic and poetic appeal of the Huangshan has not kept it from the hands of developers. Since my "epic" crawl up the stone steps, the government has installed three cable cars to whisk tourists to the tops of the peaks or to areas where hiking trails lead to special outlooks guaranteed to offer superb photo opportunities.

And finally, on a recent trip to southwest China I discovered a most unusual means of accommodating tourists. After seeing the movie, *Avatar*, the demand for visiting the actual place where the strange rock formations were filmed has increased tenfold. The government installed an outdoor elevator to take visitors to the top of one of the pinnacles so that they can take photos of what they had already seen in the move.

I find the Disney effect a blight on the ancient sites that are interesting in their own rights. But apparently the new tourists – the Chinese tourists who are just now discovering their own country – love the plastic garish additions to their sightseeing experiences.

Dare To Do It!

Chinese roofline in the Forbidden City.

1980 Tiananmen Square with portraits of Lenin and Stalin.

Dare To Do It!

Nancy at the Great Wall, 1980.

The Great Wall before Restoration.

On top of Huangshan.

Climbing the stairs to the top of Huangshan took two days.

Dare To Do It!

The stairs seemed to go up forever. Note the people climbing in the distance at the top of the photo.

Xian farmers going to market.

Dare To Do It!

This 1980 photo shows an ancient teahouse that is still standing in Old Shanghai.

INDIA

By the end of summer I was back home happy to see Jim and the kids. While I was away, Jim had become totally immersed in the children's lives. That was a good thing because I usually took care of all of their basic needs.

I was too busy to think of travel as the kids were now in high school and so busy with activities it seemed like rush hour at our house. Jim and I were always running here and there and trying to attend all the functions in which they were involved. At that time Jim and I were also teaching skiing and had to be in the mountain by early Saturday mornings. We would go to our daughter's basketball games on Friday nights, then drive three hours to the ski resort, where we then hiked in the dark up the side of the mountain to a cabin where we spent the night. The next morning we got up early to make a few ski runs on the pristine snow before the buses arrived with all the people taking lessons. We taught a couple of classes and then had the rest of Saturday and all day Sunday to ski. After the two days of skiing, we would pile into the car and head home to get ready for the work week. If the children were free, they came with us; otherwise, they would stay with friends with whom they attended school.

At this time, the school district had decreed that all teachers had to have a master's degree in order to advance on the pay schedule, or salaries would be frozen. I wanted to be at the top of the salary scale by the time I retired since my pension would be determined according to my last two years of teaching. That meant I had to return to the university. I could not afford to quit my job in order to take the required courses during the day so I had to find a degree program offered in the evenings. The one and only discipline that fit this requirement was in the business department. This was a far cry from my choices: anthropology and Asian studies. It was not possible to complete a graduate program in my chosen disciplines by attending courses in the summertime, so I had no choice but to enroll in business courses. I told myself that once I was immersed in the courses I would like them. I never felt more than lukewarm about any of them, but I could write, so I did well on all the essay assignments. I even traded my writing skills for help completing the financial problems that were too complicated for me to really understand. I was amazed at the number of graduate students who were experts at figuring out the problems but could not write coherently.

Dare To Do It!

My life became busier than ever. I taught school all day, commuted an hour to Seattle, attended a couple of classes, and drove the hour home at midnight. Somehow I managed to prepare lessons and correct papers and attend the children's activities on the weekends. Jim was a big help taking care of the children while I was gone. I remember my daughter complaining that when I came to her basketball games I was always correcting papers, and she wanted me to be more attentive. But I did what I could to be at all three kids' functions. Somehow even with the crazy schedule I managed to complete my master's within a year. The daily schedule was far from boring since I had no time to stop and think about it. It was rather ironic that I obtained a master's in finance since it required working with numbers. Math was not my best subject, and I hated pouring over financial pages. Apparently, national companies tracked graduate students because as soon as I had earned my degree, I received several calls offering me positions that would have paid me twice to three times what I received from teaching. I wasn't interested.

Once I had completed my master's I returned to the university to study Chinese language and culture. Since I was not working toward a degree, I could take just one course at a time and cut my commute dramatically, freeing me to spend more time with Jim and the children.

During the summers, many universities offered workshops or seminars that paid participants. In addition, the courses offered points depending upon the length of the course. An accumulation of points would qualify a teacher to move up on the salary scale. I took advantage of those programs that focused on Asia and the Pacific Rim. Since the courses were close to home, I could commute each day and be home in the evenings with the family.

One summer I attended a state educational conference where I heard a lecturer explain how he had traveled in the summer to various countries in the world through a government sponsored program called the Fulbright Seminar. After WWII, Senator Fulbright sponsored a bill with the purpose of strengthening cultural exchanges between educators in the United States and other countries. He wanted to develop Americans, who would become leaders in a "community of nations." Many of the Fulbright programs occurred during the academic year, but there was one summer program that would last between four and six weeks. The countries to which the participants visited would pay all expenses and thereby reduce their debt to the United States.

I listened enthralled. Here was an opportunity to travel for free, and since the program was during the summer, it would not disrupt the academic school year. With my children always gone to summer camps and Jim heavily involved in softball, I could be away for a couple of months. But there was one big problem. Since there was room for only twenty participants and half of them were university professors, only ten high school teachers would be chosen out of the entire United States. The chances of becoming part of this program were not good. Still, I decided I had nothing to lose by trying.

When I mentioned that I was applying for this coveted assignment, several of my colleagues looked at me as if I were crazy and said the usual, "Who do you think you are? You don't have a chance." I didn't bother to tell my parents about my plans since I knew they would say the same thing.

I filled out all the paperwork, sent it in and was told to be at a specific place at the university in Seattle for an interview. When I arrived I was ushered into a private room where there were just two women who were hired to screen candidates and make recommendations. One of the women was friendly and positive and clearly liked my responses to her questions. She continued to send me encouraging vibes. But the other woman was the direct opposite. She immediately attacked me for being an unfit wife and mother. She asked me how I could justify leaving my husband and children for the entire summer. She continued to hammer her negative point of view no matter what I said. I tried to explain how busy the family was and that none of them would be home during the time I would be away. But she didn't like any of my answers. After the interview on my way home I tried to remember if I said anything that would lead to a positive outcome, but it seemed obvious that a positive and a negative canceled each other out. My chances were nil. And several weeks later I received the letter that told me I had not made the cut.

I thought about the program and it still sounded so appealing that I decided I would apply again. When I looked at the countries offering the summer Fulbright programs for the next year, it looked as if all of them were specifically geared to social studies teachers since their focus was on history or politics. I was about to discard the material when I noticed a single seminar available for teachers of the humanities. It went to India. High school English courses have been set in stone for years with the senior year devoted to British literature, the junior year to American literature and the sophomore year devoted to world literature, but, in fact, was basically European with a section of Japanese haiku. There was no literature that addressed Asia or the Middle East. I knew very little about India except for Gandhi since he was always mentioned in American Literature when reading about Martin Luther King Jr.

I didn't know if it was my resume, my letter of application or the interview that was the disqualifying factor, but I decided I needed to revise the first two before applying again. As I thought about what I could do to increase my chances, it dawned on me that I had lots of room for improvement. Each year I included in my writing class a section on careers, showing students how to write a resume and a letter of application. I stressed the importance of doing research whether the student was interested in college or in obtaining a job. I told them that they needed to find out what the college or company was looking for in an applicant. I realized that I had not done this on my own application. I knew what the Fulbright program was, but I had no idea what the organization was looking for in terms of participants.

I began looking for teachers who had already been a part of the program. I wrote letters asking them to describe what they thought were the reasons they had been chosen. After communicating with a number of these teachers, I learned that the committee was looking for people who were involved in educational activities on the state and national level. I had no such experience.

I had been the advisor to a multicultural club, in which I basically handled any problems exchange students had. Occasionally, a Japanese student attended our school, but for the most part the students were all from European countries. The club was relatively small, but we raised enough money each year for the students to visit Vancouver, British Columbia. Still, I needed to find additional ways to show my leadership in cultural activities beyond the school setting.

At this time the school was receiving many Vietnam students and those that I got to know in class often shared some of their problems adjusting to American life. As far as I could tell, no one in the school district was doing anything extra to help them. I decided to start a district-wide multicultural committee to address the needs of all minority students enrolled in our system. I invited interested teachers and administrators to join our discussions, and even enlisted the assistant superintendent, who as an African-American lady, wanted to see more support for African-American students. The committee met once a month to discuss problems and their solutions related to minority students. These recommendations were then sent to the school board, and in some cases our suggestions were able to influence the board to action. Overall, the program resulted in some positive changes throughout the district. In fact, the assistant superintendent was so pleased with the results that she asked me to quit teaching and join her to develop a series of lectures detailing ways districts could provide assistance to minority students. I had to turn her down because there was no guarantee of an income from the lectures, and with three children in college or headed in that direction, I could not afford to give up my paycheck for an uncertain future.

I made contact with social studies teachers who were involved in state and national conventions and offered my services. I also gave speeches at these conventions describing China right after the Cultural Revolution. Lots of teachers were interested since few if any had been to China in 1980. It wasn't easy getting up in front of my colleagues to talk so I did the logical thing. I brought along slides that I had taken. With the lights dimmed and everyone focused on the photos, I was able to relax and talk without appearing nervous, as I definitely was. Someone in the audience might have traveled to China in the three years since I had been there, but I knew that it was unlikely than anyone would have been in China when I visited. I also had the advantage of having stayed in China for two and one-half months while most people visiting would have come on a two-week tour that would have provided less insight into the Chinese culture as it was then. It was gratifying to find a relatively large audience interested in my experience, and it gave me the needed confidence to speak at more school district functions.

The winter of 1985 I applied to the Fulbright program again with my revised resume and letter of application. I heard nothing, and by the beginning of May the school year was winding down so I assumed I had been rejected a second time. Then in the middle of the month I received a phone call during one of my classes. I worked in an annex far removed from the central office of the high school, and when I had to step outside the classroom momentarily I was not in a good mood. The students were occupied in discussion groups so leaving briefly was not a problem, but when the person on the phone asked me if I wanted to go to India, I told him his joke was not funny and I hung up. Since many of my colleagues knew I had applied again for the Fulbright, I figured one of them had gone to the main office and called me as a prank. Luckily the person who had called rang me again later in the day and amused at my reaction, assured me that he was calling from Washington, D.C. and was seriously inviting me to join the group going to India that summer. I wanted to believe him, but it wasn't until I received a packet of material along with an acceptance letter that I finally felt excited. It seemed incredible that I had been chosen. The person who called on behalf of the Fulbright committee told me that the members had been too busy to conduct interviews so they decided to take those persons who had come in second the year before.

After a flurry of preparations I headed to Columbia University to meet the group with whom I would be traveling. I was so eager to be on time I flew into New York City a day early. One of the other participants a little round lady from Florida was already there. She invited me to join her that next morning at church services. Trying to be agreeable, I said I would go with her. The next morning we took the subway to the lower Eastside of Manhattan and entered a small church that held only about a hundred people. It turned out to be a haven for gay theater people, who were extremely talented and performed songs and poetry readings that were exceptionally lovely. Afterward, my new teacher friend invited me to join her in walking in the gay parade that started at the church and wound its way through the city. We linked arms and walked for several miles before it was time for the two of us to return to Columbia for a reception that evening. I was so surprised that this nondescript little woman would lead me on such a great adventure.

That evening I met the other participants in the program. As they introduced themselves I found myself in complete shock. A majority of them were published authors or artists. Many had doctorates, even though high school teachers needed only a masters to teach. My roommate was the only one absent from the reception, but she had a good reason. She was California's choice for the "Teacher-in-Space" program and was in Washington D.C. being interviewed for next year's flight. Because California is a highly influential state, she was sure that she would be the teacher heading into space. As it turned out, the committee for the space program decided to choose a teacher from a small school district, and my roommate was out of luck. At least she felt that way then, but, in reality, she was very lucky since the following year that spacecraft blew up in a horrific accident.

My roommate arrived just as we were heading for the airport to fly to India. She, like the other participants, was very impressive. She had her doctorate in law but decided to teach on the high school level where she felt she would have the best opportunity to make a difference in teenagers' lives. At first I felt intimated, but keeping my mouth shut and letting her do the talking worked well, and we both got along just fine. She described the grueling interviews she had experienced in Washington D.C. and then went on to talk about the work she did in her school district and how she was the president of the teacher's union and, with her law degree, kept the school board on its toes. When she asked me about my background, I mumbled a few sentences and then asked her what subjects she taught. That diversion worked well because she clearly liked to talk about her teaching methods and how her students left her classes so well prepared that they all were accepted to college. I thought about some of my students, like the young man I found outside my classroom high on drugs trying to climb the flagpole, or the student who shot and killed his best friend over the weekend over an argument. We certainly had different kinds of students.

She had honors students, and I had students who were more interested in working after high school, although this fact alone would not necessarily make one group more susceptible to crime than another. No matter what our differences were, we did share a sense of adventure that worked well for both of us during the seminar.

As I learned more about the people with whom I was traveling my parents' favorite phrase popped into my head: "Who do you think you are?" Indeed, I had to wonder who I was that I would be included with these accomplished educators. There must have been a mistake, and I was inadvertently included on the roster. At first, I worried that someone would realize I was an imposter and tell me to pack up and go home, but, until I was booted out, I decided to keep my mouth shut and not display my ignorance. I was especially impressed with the college professors who clearly knew a lot about India. I listened and took notes hoping to expand my knowledge when I returned home, and I quickly filled three notebooks with major topics on the culture of the country. There was so much I didn't know; it was overwhelming. Still, I decided I would try to absorb as much as I could and fill in the gaps in the future.

After landing at the New Delhi airport we were met by our Indian guide and with his help cleared customs and boarded a minibus for our ride into the city to our hotel. We traveled along a well-maintained highway that soon morphed into an urban avenue lined with modern buildings. At first the view out the window was of relatively nondescript rural countryside, but as we approached the city a shantytown appeared. It went on for miles. There were lean-tos and cardboard shacks and sheets of plastic propped up on sticks. The narrow paths that wound through the town looked muddy due to a stream of water that flowed nearby. It was difficult to tell what the people were like since the bus passed by so quickly. All I could see were brightly clad women wrapped in saris, (curtain-like material that they wrapped about their bodies and draped over their shoulders and heads). I blinked each time my eyes caught the flashes of bright light reflected off the bangles worn on their arms and legs. The living conditions were deplorable, and yet the women were dressed in brilliant colors looking cheerful and gay as if going to a party.

We arrived at our hotel set inside a walled compound with guards at the entrance. It was clearly a modern five-star hotel. I was amazed at the pristine gardens outside the building and the sanitary white décor indoors. It was as if we had entered another world in contrast to the dirty, dusty and unkempt road outside the compound. I had never stayed in such a luxurious place. The tastefully decorated room with two king sized beds, double sinks and a bathroom the size of a our living room at home was certainly delightful to experience, but seemed excessive. Why would anyone need all that space for just sleeping overnight? The room was sterile; it had no personality. I preferred older buildings whose walls, could they speak, would tell interesting histories of people and events that had happened there.

The first evening in the city we were taken to the American Embassy for a reception in our honor. Perhaps the other participants felt it was their due, but I couldn't help feeling that I was still an imposter. What kind of intelligent conversation could I carry on amidst these important people? As it turned out the ambassador's wife was very gracious and immediately made me feel at ease. She seemed interested in my focus on women's role in Indian society. As I walked about the immaculate gardens that surrounded the embassy I couldn't help but think of all those poor people living in the slums on the edge of the city. I found the contrast profoundly disturbing, but even so, I had to admit that the country was one of the most fascinating in the world.

The Hindu religion was based on thousand-year old myths, and yet the gods of those stories remained a large part of people's daily lives. At the same time, the Muslim religion was also well established in India, and the people who followed this religion had a completely different set of values. Those who practiced these two major religions, or even one of several minority religions, wore clothing or practiced rituals that visibly displayed their beliefs. This seemed to be so different from America where people generally kept their religious beliefs private. Sometimes the Hindus and the Muslims provoked each other, and newspaper accounts would detail a burning of a mosque or a Hindu temple, which then would lead to major conflicts wiping out entire villages.

As soon as the group was settled, we began the first of a series of seminars. Sometimes, historians talked about living under British rule and the conditions that led to the country's independence. At other times professors read their works and discussed Indian authors, who have made an impact on Indian society. I vividly remember an author who read a story entitled *The Boss Who Came to Dinner*. The story's focus was on the cultural problems that arise when persons from different societies make assumptions about each other and then act accordingly, often with negative results. Having grown up in a rural community in America, I had taken for granted that everyone loved America and would want to live there if they could. I was shocked to discover that there are people in the world who actually did not agree! How could that be? Many Indians thought their way of life was better for a number of reasons. They often mentioned the narrow mindedness of Americans, who were so xenophobic. I knew my parents were not open-minded about foreigners, but I really had never discussed the idea with my friends or colleagues. Now I was confronted with completely new perspectives. It was a profound awaking.

Some lectures dealt with the reasons for the frequent clashes between Muslims and Hindus, but only once was the problem of poverty brought up and then quickly dismissed. When I had the opportunity I asked our Indian guide to help me understand why there were so many slums, and what was being done to help these people improve their lives. He said that most educated Indians preferred to ignore the problem. He said that for thousands of years, Indian society had a rigid caste system. This meant that people were segregated into a particular social group, the intellectuals and teachers at the top and the Dalits, untouchables, at the bottom. Rarely could one move up the hierarchy. When the country achieved independence, the caste system was outlawed. However, many Indians still believed in the value of a stratified society, particularly for the Dalits, who were still facing discrimination some forty years later.

Our group was invited to meet Rajiv Gandhi, the prime minister of India. That would have been a memorable event, but the morning we left for our meeting we found the entire city locked down with soldiers at every intersection stopping all traffic. A member of parliament had been assassinated during the night, and our meeting was canceled. Given the number of high profile government officials who have been killed in India, one has to wonder why anyone would want to go into politics.

After the seminars were finished each day, my roommate and I would go out to explore Old Delhi. New Delhi with its high rises and modern hotels was a typical large city much like any urban center in the world, but Old Delhi had character. The cacophonous chaos on the streets was deafening and a bit overwhelming. People carried out their routine lives right on the sidewalks: a man might be having his beard trimmed, getting a haircut, or having his shoes repaired. We had to weave our way among the various groups of men squatting and smoking in animated conversation. Interestingly there were few women on the streets, presumably because they were expected to be at home tending to domestic duties. This was, after all, Old Delhi, where most of the people were skilled labors with little formal education and where they lived according to the traditions handed down from one generation to the next.

It didn't seem possible that there could be so many people packed into the narrow winding streets. It just was beyond anything one could possibly see in America. Not knowing in which direction we were heading, we often found ourselves lost, but that was the fun of exploring. When we decided it was time to return to the hotel, we simply flagged down an auto rickshaw, a three wheeled motorized vehicle with open sides, no safety belts and no shocks. The ride through the old city was especially jarring on the uneven cobblestone streets. Riding in the rickshaws was much like riding an amusement park ride. The start and stops were often accompanied by sudden jerks that could throw you off balance if you were not holding on. It was pleasant to feel a breeze blow through the vehicle cooling us in the ninety-degree temperature, but, at the same time, we had to breathe the thick black fumes from all the traffic in the street.

The persons in charge of planning the seminar in India tried to cover every facet of Indian life: history, politics, religion, and the arts. They combined the seminars with travel to many parts of the country. So, after our initial stay in Delhi, we headed off to many historical sites. Earlier, I had mentioned being overwhelmed with all the information presented to us, and apparently the Indian government recognized this as a problem for all the participants because one day they presented us with detailed bibliographies on every phase of Indian culture and asked us to choose some forty books that we would like to take home. Once we had given our choices to the authorities, they told us they would pack them up and send them to our homes.

The first trip outside of Delhi was to the Taj Mahal. I didn't need to know any history to appreciate the beauty of this magnificent tomb. We arrived in Agra, a crowded dusty city of shops with wares spilling out into the streets. But when we walked through the gate that led to the Taj, the contrast was dramatic. Standing at the entrance the building seemed like a mirage shimmering in the hazy sunshine. To reach the building we had to walk a long paved walkway decorated with plants and reflecting pools. At first the building simply looked like plain white marble, but up close the walls were inscribed with abstract designs and delicate calligraphy depicting verses from the Koran. The inside walls were also highly decorated but also included inlay work using semi-precious stones. Words did not exist to describe the beauty of this architectural wonder. It simply had to be seen to be appreciated. Perhaps I found the tomb especially appealing because of its tragic history. The Mughal emperor, Shah Jahan, built the monument to honor his wife after her death, but within a few years his son came into power and imprisoned his father in Agra Fort, where Shah Jahan was able to see his wife's tomb but could never visit.

After leaving the Taj Mahal we traveled to Fatehpur Sikri, an ancient city built by the emperor Akbar. The emperor, having listened to a Sufi saint, built his capital on a rocky outcrop without considering the availability of water. Shortly after the complex of temples and palaces were built, the water supply dried up and the city was abandoned. Today, the ruins are fascinating to see, especially the Jama Mosque, one of the largest in India. When we arrived at this site I had no idea of the significance of what I was seeing. I remember being impressed by the elaborate marble screens that made it possible for women to look out without being seen from the outside. I must be a romantic because the intricate passageways that led from the harem to the emperor's chambers looked like something out of a fairy tale. Of course, the reality was that the women were treated as property and had no rights. The only women who faired in those days were the very few the emperor married. But the majority of the women were simply at the mercy of the ruler. Outside on one side of the palace was a large patio marked off like a chessboard. When the emperor wanted to play, he sat on an elevated platform and selected the most attractive young women from his harem to act as chess pieces to move wherever he directed them.

After returning to Delhi for a day, we traveled to Rajasthan. This desert area of India was one of my favorite places to visit. The people we saw as we drove to our next destination wore florescent pink turbans and saris. Often the materials used for the saris had tiny mirrors embedded in them, so that as we passed a group of women walking along the road, their dresses sparkled in the sunlight. They looked so pretty and carefree, but with huge loads of firewood, or large bundles perched on their heads, it was clear that they lives were filled with hard work, not parties.

I asked our Indian guide if we could visit a maharajah's palace, since as an elementary student, I remember reading about these wealthy rulers who rode around on elephants, wore colorful jewels and lived in such magnificent buildings. Before independence, there were many maharajahs, who owned large tracts of land and lived opulent lives amassing fortunes, hunting tigers and holding royal processions with beautiful dancing girls. Of course, as a child I did not know that those same maharajahs decimated most of the tiger population of India and that the gorgeous dancers were slaves. Once the country gained its independence, the maharajahs lost their power, and some of their wealth. To offset the cost of continuing to live in the elaborate palaces, many of the maharajahs have turned their homes into hotels. The palaces were generally composed of a series of buildings so that these former rulers and their families could still live in their homes, while the visitors stayed in another area of the complex far enough removed to give the owners privacy.

Our Indian guide said he would arrange for us to stay in a former palace when we visited Jaipur. The Rambagh Palace Hotel was everything about which I had fantasized as a small girl reading the folk tales from, *One Thousand and One Nights*. Although our accommodations were updated small rooms much like any well appointed modern hotel room, there were other rooms for the very wealthy that were magnificently appointed. As we toured the hotel we came across one bedroom that was so large my entire house could fit inside. A gold curtain hung from the canopy and elaborate pillows, cushions and thick Oriental rugs gave the appearance of stepping into a harem from yesteryear. The only thing missing was a dancing girl and some Indian music.

Adding to the mystical atmosphere was the snake charmer sitting just outside the room on the lawn. As soon as we approached, he began playing his strange woodwind instrument and the tinny sound aroused a snake that was inside a basket next to him. Slowly a magnificent cobra lifted itself some three feet straight up and then swayed back and forth as if in a trance. I was mesmerized by its beauty, like an exquisite piece of sculpture. It had a creamy yellow throat and an olive textured body whose skin gleamed in the sunlight. As I leaned forward to study this creature it occurred to me that this was just like an episode of *Animal Planet*: the cobra rises itself vertically, flares its hood, hisses and then suddenly strikes. I jumped back wondering if the charmer really had the snake hypnotized and under his control. I looked around to find that all the members of my group had disappeared, and I was the only one left to pay the gratuity the snake owner expected. But I didn't mind because the charmer's presence just added to the old world atmosphere of the hotel. I dug in my purse and gave the charmer a chunk of money and as quickly as it touched his hand, he was gone.

While we were in Jaipur we visited the Amber Fort, which is situated high on a hill and required us to hike up the long entrance way or, better still, ride an elephant. To add to my *One Thousand and One Nights* fantasy, I choice to ride the elephant. It turned out to be a slow plodding process as my elephant followed along in a long line of elephants giving tourists rides to the top of the hill. I thought that I was a more seasoned traveler now and would resist the obvious tourist overpriced "carnival ride" attraction, but the fantasy of the old folk tales had been so attractive it was wonderful to suspend reality even for just a little while. Later, when I reflected upon the visit to Rasjasthan I felt conflicting emotions. This wasn't the first time India would present opposite aspects of its culture. First, there were the extreme differences between those with great wealth and those who lived in the slums, and now there was the difference between my enjoyment of an activity that I knew was an abuse of animal rights. If I truly believed in my ideas, why was I staying in luxury hotels, like the maharajah's palace? Why was I watching a cobra held captive in a basket and made to perform for me, and why was I riding an elephant? I had been seduced by India, especially, Rasjasthan. I began to question just how strong I believed in my convictions, and that forced me to consider just who I really was, a question my parents had asked me over and over again.

We traveled on to Bombay, (now called Mumbai). Here was another lively city filled with masses of people jamming the streets with their daily routines. Because the city was so compressed since it sat on a peninsula, everything seemed denser and more chaotic than Delhi. Here was the most populous city in the country with the largest slum in Asia. I was totally perplexed. I didn't understand then (and I still do not understand) why the government could not find a means of giving the poor people a better standard of living. Long after my visit in 1985, the movie, *Slumdog Millionaire*, played throughout America and India. Many well-known Indians saw it, yet the lives of those poor people have not changed. Equally important was the publication of the book, *Behind the Beautiful Forevers*, by Katherine Boo. The book that won the 2014 National Book Award tells the story of families living in poverty next to luxury hotels near the airport. With over a million people living in the slums how could it be that at least some of these people had not seen their lives improved? I saw the slums in 1985 and thirty years later people were still living in poverty.

One evening, our group was invited to visit with Shashi Kapoor, a member of a family of famous Indian actors. Shashi was very popular at the time of our visit not only in India but internationally because he had starred with Julie Christie, a British superstar of the sixties, in the film, *Heat and Dust*. The movie told the story of a young English woman, who visited India, and met a man with whom she had an affair. Indian movies at that time were very romantic, but when it looked as if the main characters were about to become intimate, they would break into song or the female lead would dance suggestively. Kissing was a rare occurrence, so when Shashi, an Indian heart throb, kissed the English girl in the film *Heat and Dust*, it was a topic of conversation that was in the news off and on for months.

Naturally, all the women in our group were excited to meet this famous movie star. When we arrived at the high rise where he lived, we encountered bodyguards at the elevator who escorted us to the penthouse where the doors opened directly into his apartment. The floor-to-ceiling glass windows provided panoramic views of the city. After we were settled in his living room, he entered on crutches. Every female in the room must have felt like I did. I wanted to rush over and help him to the seat next to me so that I could just stare at his gorgeous face. He seemed to be perfection itself with his immaculate dress, manicured fingernails and carefully coiffed hair.

Dare To Do It!

A woman in our group, who was sitting near the entranceway, stood up and invited Shashi to sit next to her. As she fawned over him I rationalized that it was better that he was sitting across from me where I could stare at him until his eyes met mine and he would jump up and say, "Darling, where have you been all my life. Let me whisk you away on my magic carpet to my kingdom far away." I can't help it. I am a romantic!

Shashi explained that he had broken his foot in the last monsoon. The rain had been so heavy that street grates were removed to minimize the flooding. Wading through the water, he did not see the open storm drain and he fell into the hole. Luckily, people came to his rescue or he would have been swept away in the underground sewers. Apparently, each year at least a couple of unlucky souls lose their lives in this manner. For the next hour we sat enthralled while he talked about his movie career and his experiences filming. When we were leaving he shook our hands. I suppose the other women didn't wash their hand for weeks. I didn't.

Since I had decided to focus on women's role in Indian society, I asked our Indian guide if he could arrange for me to interview women from different walks of life. One of the women I talked to was quite candid in discussing her Hindu religion. I found the elaborately decorated temples and the many statues of various gods confusing. I tired to learn the names of the gods and their symbolic meaning, but it was difficult. Of course, she explained that Hindus growing up in the religion learned two ancient epics, the *Mahabarata* and the *Ramayama*. These stories were presented over and over again so that everyone, including people who were illiterate, knew the folk tales backward and forth. Every year these epics were enacted by traveling groups of thespians, who took their productions to small villages in rural areas, so, in effect, they continued the tradition of oral story telling that has been around since ancient times. I was particularly intrigued by the god, Ganesh, a pot-bellied entity with an elephant head. This seemed a weird object of worship until I learned the symbolism related to the god. Apparently the elephant head represent intelligence, but I never entirely understood why the god was sitting on a rat. But Ganesh was just one of the many gods who represented moral codes and idealist goals for which all Hindus should strive.

I wanted to know about the ritual of cremation. Hindus believe the soul must be freed of its physical being so it can begin a new journey of reincarnation as another life form. Ideally, a dying person would go to Varanasi to stay in an ashram, a holy place, near the Ganges River, the holiest river in India. When the person died his relatives performed a cremation ceremony and then scattered the ashes in the river. Although the cremation took place outside, it was a private affair. Most tourists had never seen a dead body burning and their first reaction was to record the event on film to show the folks at home. They did not think about the fact that it was a religious ritual that should not be photographed out of consideration for the people involved in paying their last respects to a loved one. At the time that our group was visiting India, the government was trying to curtail the gawkers, but with little success. If tourists couldn't film the event from the riverside, they hired boats and floated down the river until they were close enough to get that Kodak moment with their telephotos lenses. The woman I interviewed clearly explained the ceremony and its symbolism so I could understand the thinking behind the event. What I could not understand was why the tourists ignored the requests to put away their cameras and took pictures anyway.

I asked the women I was interviewing about the cows that wandered the streets of most towns and cities. Like many people I thought that Hindus worshiped cows, but that was not the case. She said that cows symbolized all living things, and, therefore, they were to be honored. Anyone harming a cow could end up in jail. I saw cows with holy marks on their foreheads indicating someone had blessed them, but, at the same time, the cows looked as if they were starving. Their ribs were so pronounced that the animals looked as if someone had stretched their skin over their skeletons. My interviewee said that people fed them, but if that were the case, the cows should have looked healthy, and all the ones I saw looked emaciated.

Another concept that I asked the woman to explain was the existence of sadhus, holy men. She explained that these men gave up all worldly things and spent their time meditating, praying, and doing yoga. They wandered the country living on handouts that people gave them in hopes their generosity would put them in good religious standing. Most sadhus were distinctively recognizable by their saffron robes, long beards, dreadlocks, and symbolic face paint. Many of them carried tridents and wore prayer beads. Their holy status enabled them to acquire free cannabis that they claimed had religious significance. Becoming a sadhu required some religious training, but for many foreigners it appeared to be worthwhile as I saw several Caucasian young men dressed as sadhus, wandering about with sunburnt skin and spaced-out expressions on their faces.

After Bombay, we travel south to Madras (now called Chennai), famous for its Carnatic music. This traditional style was extremely complicated and was performed by a small ensemble of musicians. The concerts we attended lasted a couple of hours and to my untrained ear seemed extremely repetitious and long. I found the classical dancing more appealing because the stories depicted by the performers were conveyed through gestures that helped me follow the plot, although, even then, I am sure I missed some of the action especially when one scene seemed to be happening at night and the next instance the dancers were celebrating the noontime sun. Both the music and dance were melodious but not at all like Western music. It was nice to have been exposed to them, but I could see that learning to appreciate the intricacies of these performances was an acquired taste.

We flew north to Calcutta (now known as Kolkata) next. My first impression was of masses of people much greater than I had seen in any of the other cities we had visited. It also appeared to be one of the poorest. Elegant old colonial buildings sat next to the most desperate looking slums I had ever seen. It seemed impossible for Calcutta to be so congested with people, and, yet, I could look in any direction and see a dense crowd so tightly packed together that individual faces and figures simply blended into the masses. We had no time for individual exploration, but had we found ourselves on any given street we would have been swallowed up by the crowds, and, by shear momentum, be forced to go wherever the people were headed. Instead, we spent our time talking with authors and poets, statesmen and intellectuals exchanging ideas covering every gamut of Indian culture. I should amend that last statement to say that the group engaged in lively conversation while I listened as usual and took copious notes.

My only memory of Calcutta's landmarks was the Victoria Memorial, a huge marble monument that gleamed in the hazy sun. Although it was impressive because of its shear size, what really stood out as the best memory of the city was visiting Mother Theresa's mission for the destitute and dying. When we arrived at the compound there were groups of poor people standing outside in ragged outfits holding babies or tiny toddlers. Presumably, they hoped that Mother Theresa would have pity on them and attend to their children, but the large gate was closed and locked.

When we arrived we were escorted through a small side door. Several nuns were lined up to greet us and then took us on a brief tour of a couple buildings, but we were told we could not go to the rest of the compound where the children who were close to death were housed. I thought the children we did see looked listless and sad and far from healthy. It was a gut wrenching experience. How could there be such misery in the world, especially for tiny children. It was hard to keep my emotions in check, and I couldn't help but question the existence of a higher being who would allow this to happen. Seeing the children in person made the issue real in contrast to watching pictures on television or seeing photos in newspapers where one could turn the channel or the pages and put it out of one's mind.

I will never forget just standing there in the compound after visiting the "healthy" children and, as we said our goodbyes to the nuns, looking into their care worn faces and thinking that if not for these women the children would die out in the street alone and unloved. We had been told that we would meet Mother Theresa, but unfortunately, she had not returned from a trip she had taken outside the country. Her forthcoming sainthood could not go to a more deserving person since she had created many missions throughout the world just like the one we visited whose sole purpose was to help the less fortunate.

The visit was such a moving experience we all pulled out huge wads of money to contribute to the mission. We had been told when we first arrived in India that we were not to give money to the child beggars because they belonged to gangs whose leaders kept the money. It was suggested that if we wanted to help the poor to donate to Mother Theresa's mission. Thus, we all were prepared to give a lot of money for such a good cause. I am sure the other members of our group felt the same heart wrenching experience as I did and gave all the money they could spare.

Thinking about the visit later, I had to question what I could do to help people living in poverty, especially the children. Over the years I had given money at times of disaster and then to only select organizations. The numerous reports of administrators at the top of the charities being rewarded with huge salaries and little going to the actual cause had turned me off to donating on a regular basis.

Having visited Mother Theresa's mission, I was inspired to do some research to find other charities like hers whose focus was on those in need rather than on the administrators. While I preferred to donate to organizations that helped third world countries, where the poverty was so prevalent, I also resolved that on my return to American I would donate some of my time to a worthy charity in my local community. I had talked about doing this for years but never could find the time. I decided to make a bigger effort.

After our visit to Calcutta we returned to Delhi where the summer seminar was about to end. Before we said our goodbyes we had one last visit to make to an important site of monumental significance. We were taken to the Raj Ghat on the Yamuna River where Mahatma Gandhi was cremated. The memorial was a loving tribute to a man who used non-violent protest to inspire millions of people to demonstrate against the British government eventually leading to India's independence. Gandhi's ideals have inspired people throughout the world including Martin Luther King, Jr., who used non-violent protest in his work for civil rights. Standing in front of the plinth made Gandhi's philosophy seem more real than reading about his beliefs in textbooks or seeing an old grainy film of an event that happened so long ago. Looking at the eternal flame and the flowers strewn in loving memory seemed to give life to his teachings, and I felt inspired to make more of my life. I had to admire a man who was willing to go to jail for his beliefs. It made me question whether I had any convictions for which I would be willing to stand up and fight or was I like most people who talked about their intentions but never put their words into action. I wasn't sure. It was a dilemma because, like most people, I didn't live in a vacuum, and my decisions and actions impacted my loved ones.

At our last meeting together the director of the program handed each of us an envelope that contained several hundred dollars in Indian rupees. I was speechless. What should I do with this windfall? I could take it home, or I could extend my educational experience for another week or two before having to be back at school. After talking it over with my roommate we decided to visit Nepal. Since the flight from Delhi to Katmandu was only an hour and thirty minutes, we could easily spend a week there before flying home to return to our teaching jobs.

The first flight we could arrange left that afternoon and dropped us in Lucknow, India where we would board a connecting flight to Katmandu the next morning. When we arrived at the airport in Lucknow, the place was very quiet with only a handful of employees wandering about. We tried to find a taxi to take us into town, but there did not seem to be any. Finally, someone suggested we go outside the airport perimeter where we could find a pedicab. We walked a half-mile to a main road and right away a pedicab operated by a gaunt looking elderly man came down the road.   We ignored his gestures hoping a motorized vehicle would show up since we did not believe in having another human being pulling us about. Unfortunately, the city was several miles away and, because it was late in the afternoon, my roommate and I had no choice but to depend upon local transportation. When no motorized vehicle showed up, we finally waved to the pedicab fellow, who had stopped a block in front of us. We walked up to his worn ancient looking carriage and climbed aboard. I showed the fellow the address of the hotel that had been recommended to us at the airport.

As we slowly crept along the road at a pace that I could match walking, we came to a hill. I jumped out of the carriage and began walking along side the vehicle. The pedicab driver looked distressed and waved to me to get back inside, but I held out until we reached the top of the hill, and it was clear that the cyclist could coast at least part of the way downhill. Staring at the back of this emaciated man, I thought that he should be riding and either my roommate or I should be pedaling his buggy. This worn down bedraggled man could have been the model for the man described in a book I had recently read called, *The City of Joy*. The authors, Dominic LePierre and Larry Collins had described the life of a pedicab cyclist and how he had come down with black lung disease, an illness common among these drivers. The authors described how the pedicab driver worked without rest day after day just to earn enough to keep his family from starving. When his daughter reached her teens he was expected to arrange a marriage for her. In order to do this he had to supply a dowry, and the better the dowry the better the daughter's marriage prospects. With no way of earning the necessary money for the dowry, he did the only thing he could do. He signed a contract with a company that gave it the rights to his bones after his death. Immediately after he died the company would claim his body, remove the skeleton and sell it to medical labs, hospitals and universities throughout the world. I couldn't help thinking that I might meet this man again as a skeleton in some doctor's office in America. What a gruesome thought!

We finally arrived at our hotel in the city proper, and when we checked in found it odd that the clerk asked us to fill out a detailed form asking us for a specific description of what we looked like, what we were wearing, what our contact information was at home, our passport numbers and a detailed outline of our plans for the evening. We had never been required to do this before, but then we never booked our hotel rooms while on the Fulbright program, so we decided that the form must be standard procedure for foreigners.

Our room was old, worn, and smelled of smoke and dried sweat. On one of the windows the sash was broken so that the thing could not be shut. Since it was so hot, we preferred the window open but just below us was a roof that someone could easily scale. The room was clearly not safe should someone want to get in, although I don't know why I worried about the window when the door to the room looked so thin that one swift kick would probably knock it down. The bathroom had broken tile, a cracked mirror and yellow water stains in the sink. I remember looking at the sagging bed with the dingy sheets and threadbare blanket and comparing it to our pristine luxury rooms we had occupied while on the Fulbright. When we first arrived at our hotel in Delhi at the beginning of the seminar, I had commented on our luxury accommodations and how unnecessary and extravagant these were and how I would have preferred to stay in an older hotel because it had more character. Well, here I was in a typical Indian hotel, but it had neither character nor charm.

Dare To Do It!

From the little we had seen of the city, it did not look to be a tourist destination. We saw no foreigners, nor were there any staying at the hotel. When we went downstairs to go out to a restaurant for dinner, the clerk behind the desk expressed great concern. I can't recall if he actually said it was not safe, but he certainly conveyed the impression. He told us to wait while he made a phone call. A few minutes later a policeman appeared who spoke English. He said he would escort us to the restaurant for dinner and that when we were finished we were to have the restaurant call a taxi for us.

As we left the hotel and walked the few blocks to the restaurant, we noticed that there were only men on the streets. Maybe it was not appropriate for women to be alone at night on the streets. It didn't help that there were no streetlights and the only source of light was from the businesses lining the street. This left everything in shadow. The hotel clerk, the policeman and the dark masses of men milling around made both my roommate and I feel very uncomfortable, so we were very happy to enter a well-lit restaurant with lots of men and women seated at the various tables. Apparently it was okay for women to be out at night if they had male escorts. My roommate and I were the only females without companions.

After we had eaten we asked the waiter to call a taxi for us. It took over thirty minutes for a cab to show up, but at least we were able to ride back to the hotel in safety. That night we both found it difficult to sleep. The paper-thin walls allowed us to hear footsteps going back and forth overhead and voices talking as if in the same room. In addition, the screeches, yelling and shouting going on in the street seemed to go on all night. We both were up very early in the morning ready to head back to the airport.

The flight from Lucknow to Kathmandu was short and by noon we were in Nepal. We found a light airy room, with plain but serviceable furnishings, including a comfortable bed with crisp white sheets and a tiny but sparkling clean bathroom. Here was the type of room that I thought was perfect: not fancy like our seminar luxury rooms and not sleazy like the one in Lucknow.

We stowed our bags and headed out to visit the old section of the city. We headed straight for Durbar Square where there were dozens of ancient temples, their worn wooden exteriors glowing in the afternoon sun. Along the side streets were stores selling all kinds of outdoor gear for backpackers and mountain climbers. Because so many foreigners came through Kathmandu, cafes entitled, *Mom's Apple Pie* and *Hamburger Heaven* promised the visitor treats from home. One street, called Freak Street, was filled with tiny shops selling drug paraphernalia, and clusters of young people were standing in doorways or in side streets.

Walking about the square and the alleyways nearby, I felt as if the entire place was part of some surreal fantasy. As the afternoon turned to dusk, devotees began lighting candles in the temples. The flickering light danced across the old wooden buildings while smoke from outside grills hung in oddly shaped puffs of cloud and shadows from the surrounding mountains crept along the lanes and alleyways. In the half-light we stopped at a stall and tried the lamb kabobs. They turned out to be unusually tender and moist, and my roommate and I agreed it was one of the best meals we had eaten. We checked out other stalls before heading back to our hotel room to plan the week's adventures. But as we began walking, we were surprised to see how quickly the light had disappeared from the sky and in the dark with only a few storefronts to light the way we stumbled over the uneven pavement until we finally arrived at our hotel.

The next morning we took a mini van to Bhaktapur, an ancient city just a few miles to the east of Kathmandu. The center of the city, Bhaktapur Durbar Square, had even more temples than in Kathmandu. As we passed a group of buildings we noticed that they were leaning to one side as if about to topple over. None of them looked like they had been upgraded since they were built in 1000AD. (Sadly, the 2015 earthquake did demolish all of them). Bhaktapur was even more otherworldly than Kathmandu, and, with very few tourists, we wandered about enjoying the quiet old world atmosphere.

We returned to Kathmandu and took another mini van to Boudhanath, one of the largest Buddhist stupas in the world. On top of a round dome sat a rectangular structure and on top of that was a golden spire. The four sides of the rectangle had giant eyes staring down at us. These eyes symbolized the all-seeing ability of the Buddha. As I did the traditional walk around the stupa I could feel those eyes boring into me. Everyone else, like me, walked quietly almost as if on tiptoe. The eyes were those of some stern parent making sure that those in the Buddha's presence were attentive to their devotions and acting with dignity and grace. I couldn't help but think of the times I had been in church and had nodded off when the sermon was too long. That wouldn't happen here.

We returned to Kathmandu in the late afternoon. The rest of the evening we spent talking to backpackers we encountered on Freak Street to find out if any of them knew how to get to Chitwan National Park. I had wanted to go there to see the tigers ever since I had seen an advertisement for Tiger Tops Jungle Lodge. From the photo on the ad it looked as if the lodge had been built up in the trees above a watering hole where jungle animals, including tigers came every night. What could be more exciting than to see a wild tiger up close from a tree "house?" So, after asking different groups of backpackers about traveling south to the park, we gathered the specifics we needed to leave the next morning. Naturally, we did not plan to stay at the Tiger Tops since it would be too expensive, but we hoped to find some simple accommodations nearby.

The next morning we got up very early to board a mini van that we had inspected as best we could to see that it had good tires and hopefully that meant good brakes. The van looked new compared to the many dilapidated vehicles we saw at the bus station. We didn't have to wait long before the van was full, and we headed out of the city. At first the roadway was wide and level and the ride went smoothly, but soon it narrowed into a twisting lane with hairpin turns, and the pavement disappeared altogether. As we rode further down the mountainside, we encountered vertical rock faces on one side and shear drop-offs on the other. I couldn't decide which was more frightening the hell-bent speed at which the driver negotiate the turns, or his snail like driving when we had to creep past an oncoming car and he moved the van over onto the loose gravel where the tires would sink into the soft ground making it feel as if the van was slipping off the edge of the mountain. I had visions of us floating in space for an instance before spiraling down thousands of feet to the cliffs below. It was difficult to relax.

Our erratic progress down the mountain was suddenly halted by a landslide. The road had completely disappeared. Groups of emaciated looking men using hand tools were laboring in the intense heat. Most of them wore shorts and sleeveless tee shirts and thongs. No one had any kind of safety gear. I couldn't believe these men were moving rocks and shoveling gravel wearing only thongs. Somehow, early in the day, these laborers had maneuvered huge boulders into the space where the road had once been. The men were trying to fill the gaps between the rockery with gravel, but some gaps were so large it looked as if they could easily swallow a person. It certainly didn't look safe for a van to cross. My friend and I asked the driver to let us get out so that we could walk across the landslide area, and the rest of the passengers got up and followed us out of the van. As we followed the group over the rubble, I looked back to see the driver sitting all alone in the van. As we stumbled and tripped over the uneven rocks, I could feel the boulders shifting. A bit of a chill went up my spine. What if the entire mass of rockery instantly gave way? I tried to hurry to the other side, but the jagged rocks made it difficult to proceed with any speed. I remember looking down through one of the larger gaps and involuntarily sucking in my breath. The land looked to be thousands of feet below us. The cliff was so eroded it actually looked concave so that the boulders that the men had used to fill the gaps appeared to be hanging in space. The men were trying to fill the gaps with gravel, but it looked as if the gravel simply fell completely through. I was relieved to get to the other side of the landslide area back on the roadway.

Once we reached the safety of the pavement, we all turned around and watched to see what the van driver would do. The driver gunned the motor and tried to drive up onto the first boulder. He managed to get the front wheels on top, but then he appeared stuck. The laborers ran over and began tipping the van from side to side and pushing from behind. I closed my eyes for a second thinking the van was sure to roll backwards on top of those men. The spindly legs and stick-like arms of those men must have been solid muscle because the group managed to inch the van forward until all four wheels were atop the first boulder.

The driver gunned the motor again and the van inched forward until most of it was onto the second boulder. Then suddenly the van jerked to one side and it was clear that one of the wheels had fallen into a gap. The van was now leaning at a precarious angle as if it were about to fall on its side. But the laborers scurried under the van and began pushing the vehicle upright. All this was happening while the laborers and the van driver were yelling at each other, presumably telling each other what to do. Once the van was upright, it looked as if it were suspended in the air. Nevertheless, someone produced a tire jack and managed to secure it to the bumper and began pumping the van even further up in the air. It was amazing that the van remained upright and hadn't fallen on the men. Once the wheel was airborne, a group of men produced a board, placed it over the gaping hole and lowered the wheel onto it. The driver gunned the motor and the van inched forward until all four wheels were on the second boulder. From there the driver was able to maneuver the van onto the solid roadway, but not without more rocking and shoving. When the van finally reached solid ground everyone cheered, and big grins spread over the laborers' faces. I thought the laborers would be exhausted after that, but as soon as we passengers got back in the van and the driver waved goodbye, the laborers went back to shoveling as if nothing had happened.

Apparently the precarious exercise getting the van across the landslide area made no impression on the driver because we were soon whipping around corners at ungodly speeds again. In fact, he seemed to have speeded up. Fortunately, after surviving several more hairpins curves and close encounters with oncoming traffic, we made it to the lower part of the mountain where the road leveled off, and we began traversing rolling hills that morphed into flatter areas of grassland. We traveled for another hour or two and finally came to a fork in the road where there was a bench and what appeared to be a bus sign. The driver stopped and motioned for my roommate and I to get out. We had been told that at this bus stop we should wait for a local bus to take us to town. We had no idea what the name of the town was that we were going to and we had no maps.

As we stood there watching the bus disappear around a curve, I began to feel anxious. Here we were at a fork in a road with no idea where we were. On the advice of a couple of potheads, we had taken off into this unknown part of the country with just some hand-written directions on the back of an envelope. How could we have started such an adventure without even checking a map to have some idea where we were? And, on top of that, we had not told anyone that we were going to Nepal. This might have been the craziest idea I had ever had. All around us were acres of grassland. We saw no houses or buildings of any kind. And we saw nothing that even remotely resembled a jungle. I kept thinking about what someone had told us when we first arrived in India. We had been told not to go out into the countryside because the local villagers would see us as rich tourists and might rob us. In the past, independent travelers had been beaten, tied up and thrown down wells to disappear forever. If something happened to us, no one would ever know. With those "happy" thoughts, we waited.

About a half hour went by, and finally an old, tired-looking bus came into view, and when we waved, the driver stopped, opened the doors and motioned for us to board. He kept revving the engine that coughed and sputtered and sounded as if it might quit at any moment. As soon as we were inside, he closed the doors and stepped on the gas. The bus lurched forward and then settled into a slow hiccupping ride toward the town without a name. We managed to find two seats in the back after climbing over a crate full of chickens and waiting until a woman removed her goat from one seat and a bundle of produce from another. Some of the people starred at us, clearly curious; others smiled and talked to us in their native language. Although we didn't understand them, their gestures indicated that they were trying to be friendly.

When we arrived on the outskirts of the town, we got off the bus and looked around. Local people were streaming passed us into the town carrying baskets of vegetables or pulling along various domestic animals. Presumably they were all going to a market to sell their goods. We would have enjoyed exploring the market, but we were focused on visiting the jungle and didn't have time to look at local produce since it was already early afternoon and we were still unsure which direction to go to find Chitwan National Park.

It would seem that either we got off the bus at the wrong spot, or we still had a long way to go. A jungle is pretty hard to miss, and yet, we could see nothing beyond the town but yellow unkempt grassland stretching as far as we could see.

As we stood there undecided as to our next strategy, a young boy about fourteen years old came up to us and asked, in perfect English, if he could help us.

The teen told us that his parents ran a small B&B right next to Chitwan National Park, and he would be happy to take us there. The boy seemed harmless enough, so we decided to go with him. As we walked along a dusty dirt lane, he talked about his passion for martial arts and his hero Bruce Lee. I asked him how he had learned to speak English so well, and he said he often went into the town to find foreigners and practice speaking with them because he said that to get ahead in school he needed to able to speak good English.

We walked for a couple of miles and then came to a river. Near the river's edge sat some women with parcels next to them. They had interesting tattoos on their arms, and I remember thinking that these women could easily be subjects from some National Geographic article. I tried not to stare, and it took all my willpower to keep from whipping out my camera and taking a picture. Somehow, the way the women turned away at our approach, it was clear that they would not have wanted their pictures taken.

On the further shore of the river, a man standing in a dugout canoe pushed off and poled his way toward us. When he arrived, we waded out into the water and climbed aboard the dugout, and the man began poling us across to the other side. With the weight of all the passengers, the canoe had sunk down to its gunwales, and it looked as if at any moment water would begin lapping over the sides, and we would soon be swimming, but, instead, it moved slowly forward.

As we approached the middle of the river it looked like there were several logs floating nearby, but as we got closer, it turned out that they were crocodiles. Several huge creatures were drifting along with the current and seemed to ignore the canoe that was in their path. They came so close to the canoe that I could have touched the head of one of them. Even as tingles went up and down my spine, I remember being thrilled to see these prehistoric animals up close in the wild. Apparently we were perfectly safe since the man poling the canoe ignored them, and the boy who was leading us to his parents' house just smiled.

We finally arrived at the opposite bank where we climbed out of the canoe and continued walking for another mile. As we walked the grassland began to change to lightly forested areas, but nothing looked remotely like my idea of a jungle. Finally, the young boy ran ahead and by the time we came to the small building with the thatched roof, his mother had come out to greet us. She was so young looking that it would have been easy to assume she was an older sister instead of the mother. She was very beautiful and that probably explained why the young boy was so handsome. She spoke no English so her son did all the translating.

That afternoon she made us one of the most delicious meals we had ever eaten. In just two days my roommate and I had eaten locally cooked food, and found it better tasting than any of the restaurant meals we had previously enjoyed in India.

That evening, the young boy's father showed us the sleeping huts he had built behind the main building. The huts were tiny with just a simple opening cut out of one of the mud-packed walls. The father lit a candle in the room before leaving. There was no lock on the door, but there was no need for one. We were the only visitors there. We quickly put out the candle because the thatched roof above us came down on the sides close to our beds. If that candle had accidentally fallen over, the entire hut would go up in flames. We decided that we could live without the candlelight. But we couldn't live without a toilet, so we were grateful the father had left a flashlight for our use to get to the outhouse.

In the morning after another tasty meal, we went out to find an elephant and its mahout waiting for us. The night before, the young boy had, at his father's prompting, asked us whether we wanted to walk through the jungle with a park ranger or ride an elephant. We had chosen to ride the elephant. Clearly, this was not the tourist version of elephant riding that included some kind of platform that tourists could sit on in comfort.

This elephant was outfitted with just a wide pad held on by a single piece of rope. This didn't seem to be such an important detail at first, but after we climbed up a ladder and clamored onto the elephant's back I found myself in a precarious position. The mahout was sitting on the elephant's head. My roommate climbed onto the elephant before me and managed to secure a comfortable sitting arrangement where she could dangle her legs along either side of the elephant's neck. But when I crawled up onto the broad hairy backside, and plopped down behind her, I found my legs sticking straight out. The only thing I had to hold onto was the rope securing the pad, but that did not give me any security since every time the elephant moved, I felt as if I were rolling forward or backward. Unable to bend my knees and get any kind of purchase on the animal made it difficult for me to control the motion of my body. Not only that, but stretching my legs in that manner was similar to doing the splits, an exercise I had not done since I was in grade school. Immediately, I could feel cramps in my thighs. As soon as the father had pulled the ladder away, we were off. Immediately, the pain in my upper legs became intense as the elephant moved forward. I tried to ignore the discomfort and focus on our goal of seeing a wild tiger.

At first we traveled through grasses so tall that we could easily reach out and break off the tops from our high perch. Suddenly, a noisy rustle occurred, and a huge wild pig with massive horns poking out of its face came running past. It was a good thing we had not chosen to walk! Continuing on, we came to a large body of water that might have been part of the river we had crossed earlier. As the elephant waded in, the water rose up the elephant's legs, but his belly stayed dry and so did we. We could look down and see those "logs" that were, in fact, crocodiles floating nearby. Apparently, they were no threat to the elephant.

Finally, after traversing another field of grasses, we came to the jungle. It seem so strange to be riding through tall grasses with blue sky all about us and yet be facing a wall of trees and bushes so dense and dark that it looked impenetrable. As we got closer, I thought there was no way this huge animal could walk into that mass of trees that were so close together. Then, just when we were within a few feet of the jungle, the mahout directed the elephant onto a narrow path that went inside. I had always wondered why stories set in tropical forests always described the characters as "entering" the jungle, but now it made perfect sense. It was as if we had enter through an invisible door

The elephant was too wide for the path and as the animal pushed the bushes and tree branches aside, they came swinging back hitting the sides of the elephant. I remember ducking to avoid some of the bigger branches and then peering out to the side into total darkness. How would we possible see an animal? But as our eyes adjusted, we could see tangled shrubs and trees packed together in haphazard clusters. It was so dense that there could have been hundreds of wild animals, including the tiger, just a few feet from us and we would never know.

Suddenly, a bright color caught my eye and when I looked up, I saw a snake dangling from an overhead branch. Even in the low light, sunlight filtered through the trees so that the brilliant markings on its back were clearly visible. It was stretched out vertically so that if I had reached up I could have touched its head. It was at least five feet long and about as thick as my arm. I must have cried out because just then the snake fell straight down towards me, and I remember ducking to the side as the creature grazed my foot. At the same time this was happening the mahout had turned around and was yelling at me and motioning for me to pull my feet in. Of course, I couldn't do that since I couldn't bend my knees, and I didn't need to understand his words to know that the snake must have been very dangerous. The mahout kept turning around and using his elephant hook to tap my feet. And while he was tapping my feet the elephant was moving about so I was rocking back and forth and just trying to hang on because the last thing I wanted to do was to fall off and come face to face with that snake.

We continued along the narrow path through the heavy bushes and then suddenly came out into an opening where there was a large watering hole. Standing in the muddy water was a rhinoceros with her baby.

Dare To Do It!

She was a strange looking animal with warty skin that folded about her neck and covered her body like sheets of armor. She had one huge horn in the center of her snout and funny round ears that stuck out on top of her head. Although she was no beauty, there was something majestic about her. I learned later that this particular species of rhino was heading for extinction, but that the conservationists who worked at Chitwan National Park were working on methods to protect the animals from poachers with the hopes of seeing an increase in the population in the future.

As my roommate and I fumbled in our bags locating our cameras, the rhino and her baby pushed through the dense brush and were gone. I may have gotten a photo of the rhino's rear end, but I will never know because when I had the film developed the entire roll was filled with fuzzy blotches that were supposedly animals from the jungle. Sadly, the lighting in the jungle was just too dark for good photos.

We continued traveling through the forest hoping to see a tiger, but we were not lucky. There were, however, plenty of deer crashing through the underbrush so that as we came upon them we would catch a glimpse of them disappearing so quickly that if it were not for their noisy movements, we might have imagined seeing them.

After a couple of hours we retraced our path back to the B&B where we spent the evening talking with the family as their son translated for us. The father proudly told of how he had built the main building and the small huts all by himself. The family business had been open for about a year and had many visitors from all over the world. They were clearly very hard working and happy with their lot in life. I remember thinking that we were very fortunate to have stayed with this family rather than in a fancy tourist lodge run by some big corporation.

The next morning the father had brought an ox cart pulled by two oxen and a driver to take us back to town so that we did not have to walk. While the ride was a bit rough sitting on rough wooden planks in a carriage with no springs, it was an interesting experience because the driver took us far up the river to a place where the water was low enough for the oxen to wade through, towing us along behind.

The young boy accompanied us so that he could direct us to the correct local bus. He told the bus driver that we needed to take the long distance bus back to Kathmandu and to have us get off his bus at the right place. Thus, we rode the local bus with an assortment of animals and people who all stared at us as if we were aliens. If we looked at them, they would give us a friendly smile. When we got off the bus, some of the locals even waved to us. We found ourselves back at the bus stop where we had been when we first came down the mountain. When the long distance bus came along we could see it was one of those old worn sagging vehicles looking ready for retirement. My roommate became very anxious since we had no choice but to take this bus if we wanted to get to Kathmandu that evening. As we rode along my roommate became even more nervous, and, I confess, I was a bit anxious too. We had to cross the landslide area and negotiate all those hairpin turns. But the bus could only move at a slow speed so the ride was not as frightening as it was coming down the mountain. Somehow the landslide area had been completed enough that the bus rode over the rocks without any problems and continued up the mountainside towards Kathmandu.

As we proceeded up the mountain we ran into some oncoming traffic, but now we were on the inside of the road hugging the rocky wall. That was a good thing because soon it was dark, and we were still on the road. Fortunately, few drivers were coming down the mountain, as there was no barriers along side the cliff edge so driving after dark would have been extremely treacherous. The problem with the country roads where we were was that there was no lighting along the way, so the bus headlights provided the only visibility. Luckily, by the time the night was really dark, the road had widened and we were soon inside the city limits of Kathmandu.

The next day we were able to find a direct flight from Kathmandu to Delhi where we were scheduled to fly home that evening.

When I look back at the Fulbright program for that summer I tried to think of what impressed me the most about the experience. I made a list of just those events that stood out in my memory and was surprised at how extensive it was. The visit to India taught me about a world that had previously been entirely alien to me. I felt that I had grown in confidence particularly after the seminar had ended, and I traveled independently with my roommate. We saw India from a totally different perspective from that of the seminar and that helped me to appreciate the country all the more.

Dare To Do It!

Dalits living in the streets of Delhi.

The Taj Mahal is one of the most beautiful buildings in the world.

In 1985 road construction in India was often done by manual labor.

Nancy ready to ride into Chitwan National Park looking for tigers.

Dare To Do It!

The lovely Napalese family run a small B&B next to Chitwan National Park.

ISRAEL

After returning to teaching I fell back into the old busy routine. The next several years were a whirlwind of activities as our three children graduated from high school and headed off to their respective colleges. Jim and I continued skiing in the winter and biking in the summer so there was no time to think about travel other than to visit the children wherever they were living.

After having participated in the Fulbright program, I was on the mailing list to receive brochures detailing the current programs. Each time one came in the mail I looked through it to see the offerings, and found that most were specifically targeted to history and social studies teachers. But in 1994 as I perused the listings I saw a humanities seminar that was going to Israel and Egypt. I had no real understanding of Israel and was not familiar with any literature written by Israeli authors. Egypt was a different story.

When I was in grade school our social studies class had to read about Egypt, and, like many other students in my class, I was fascinated by the pyramids, the mummies and hieroglyphics. I remember having to do an independent project building a pyramid from cardboard. I worked hard on the construction, even copying hieroglyphs on the sides. But the next morning when I was ready to head to school, I found my pyramid had collapsed into several pieces. Since it was due that day, I remember carrying the pieces into the classroom, taping the structure back together and carefully placing the pyramid on the table where the projects were to be exhibited. Then, just as the bell rang, another student came rushing into class, plopped his project down next to mine and suddenly my pyramid collapsed again. After class I asked the teacher if I could take my project home and return it the next day. She examined the sides and my carefully printed hieroglyphics and then gave me permission. I can't remember what I used to reinforce the sides so the pyramid would stay together, but I do remember being very frustrated that I was still working on the project. I didn't do much better with a group project on Egypt. My friends and I decided to dress up as mummies and took turns wrapping ourselves up in toilet paper, which quickly unraveled before the three of us could finish our task. Fortunately we had created a poster explaining the properties of mummification and that explanation saved us from a failing grade. The grade school experience may have been a bit of a disaster, but it never took away my fascination with Egypt.

Before sending in my letter of application, I tried to enhance my resume as best I could, by focusing on how I would improve my teaching by participating in the seminar. I included examples of the types of Indian literature I had added to my World Literature course after participating in the seminar to India and how I would do the same with both Israeli and Egyptian literature. I was particularly interested in exposing my students to Egyptian author, Naguib Mahfouz, because he had won the 1988 Nobel Prize for Literature. I also stressed my interest in women's role in society and my desire to meet with contemporary women authors.

When the letter of acceptance came, I was surprised because I had been told that with thousands of applicants applying each year, the Fulbright committee generally picked educators who had not been on a seminar. Since I was going to two countries for which I knew very little, I decided to do as I had in India, listen, take lots of notes, and, above all, keep my mouth shut so I didn't appear too ignorant.

I don't recall ever spending much time studying about the Middle East when I was in high school. I now had a chance to learn about a piece of land…a desert no less…that had been in conflict for thousands of years. If this were truly the Holy Land you would think it would be full of brotherly love, but, in fact, it was and still is in great turmoil. I was soon to find out just how much turmoil.

Immediately upon arriving in Tel Aviv, I saw soldiers. They were in the receiving hall of the airport; they were at the entrance and exits; they were in every side hall, nook, and bathroom - everywhere. And these men were not just parading around in uniforms, they had rifles in their hands as if ready to use at a moment's notice.

We were taken to our hotel and immediately discovered that the second floor was full of soldiers. (We were told that hotels were required to reserve the second floor for soldiers in case of any imminent threat.) Our ride to the hotel from the airport had been ordinary, and people on the streets looked calm and collected. If there was a threat, we did not see it, and the soldiers didn't act like there was one either. They wanted us to take their pictures. They wanted us to put on their jackets and hold their guns and take more pictures. Whatever threat there might have been seemed remote. That is, until the next afternoon.

We had visited an outdoor market wandering about taking photos of all the flowers, produce, crafts and especially of the older women with their weather-worn, wrinkled faces framed by colorful head scarves. They would laugh exposing gold caps on their teeth that sparkled in the sunshine when I asked to take their pictures. They were such a happy people. But several hours after we had left the market, someone detonated a bomb and blew away part of the market. The threat of conflict was real.

Later in traveling about, we were stopped by a group of protesters. Not only were they holding up signs and yelling out their issues, but also they had piled tires across the entire road and set them on fire. The thick black smoke made everyone choke and we had to turn around and return from where we had come. Since the yelling was in Hebrew, we did not understand their protests, but were told that the government was considering moving some of the settlers off the land that they now occupied but that had once belonged to the Muslims.

The Jewish man who hosted our group was an elderly person who had lived through much of Israel's history. He was so passionate, so proud and so sure that the Jewish people belonged in Israel. He was a good example of what the founding fathers of America must have been like at the start of our own country. It was a refreshing and invigorating perspective and one we would see in talking with every single citizen in the country. He talked about the beginnings of the country when the United Nations partitioned Palestine into separate Jewish and Arab states and made Jerusalem a separate entity under international control. Our host described in detail how the Arabs attacked and tried to cut off Jerusalem from the seacoast and how the Jewish people fought so passionately and finally overcame the Arabs and declared their independence. The heads of state even went so far as to declare Jerusalem its capital. Our host had fought in the war, and as he was describing it, his eyes misted, and he became emotional as he remembered his friends who had died during the conflict.

After Israel's Six Day War in 1967, the Jewish people had taken much of the Sinai Peninsula and lots of Arab territory, but after negotiations were finished, Israel agreed to remove it troops from the Sinai, but it agreed to give only a small portion of territory back to the Arabs. Instead, it began an aggressive plan to move settlers onto the land and develop it as part Israel. Israel also demolished the barriers dividing Jerusalem in half and began governing the entire city. Force may have been a temporary solution, but it did not lead to permanent peace. The Muslims sited historical evidence proving the land belonged to them. The Israelis sited historical evidence proving the land belonged to them. And so, it looked like the Holy Land would continue to be in conflict forever.

Visiting Israel was like walking through the pages of the Bible. Throughout the country no matter what direction we went we encountered references to Jesus and his teachings. But there were many references to Jewish history as well. The greatest concentration of religion was, of course, in Jerusalem.

Dare To Do It!

The Temple Mount where Abraham was planning to sacrifice his son Isaac was also the very spot where the Prophet Muhammad ascended to heaven. On top of the Mount we saw the Al-Aqsa Mosque and the Dome of the Rock, two important Muslim buildings. On one side of the Mount we visited the Western Wall, (once a part of the Second Temple) where Jews left prayers on tiny pieces of paper that they shoved into the crevices of the wall. Somehow the people of these two religions had managed to tolerate each other here in the Old City, even while their countrymen were fighting each other in some other part of the nation.

We visited the Church of the Holy Sepulchre, built on the spot where it was believed that Jesus was crucified. The interior was packed with religious devotees wanting to visit Jesus's tomb. Christian pilgrims, who had come from all over the world, walked the via Delorosa, following the path that Jesus walked bearing the cross from the Place of Judgment. The route started at the Church of the Flagellation and was marked at each of fourteen stations where some important event had occurred. The last five Stations were inside the Church of the Holy Sepulchre.

We visited the Mount of Olives, the Garden of Gethsemane and the Tomb of Mary. We also visited Mount Zion, the site of the Last Supper. As we came to each of these sites I remember how exciting it was to see the real places mentioned in the Bible. I had not studied religion since I had gone to Sunday school as a child, but I easily recognized the important places in the Holy Land.

A small group of us decided that our trip would not be complete unless we visited Bethlehem. But our government host would not go there. So we had to arrange our own transportation. I wrote a postcard to my husband about the event that went like this:

"...I had to go through a military blockade into Arab territory to visit the Church of the Nativity in Bethlehem. Our government leader would not take us, so a group of us hired a cab and went. It was a bit exciting as there are so many fanatics who are demonstrating all the time, especially now that Arafat came to Jericho. Tourists are warned to stay away from Arab Quarters and right now the Arabs occupy Bethlehem. The church is interesting, being shared by the Greek Orthodox, the Catholics and the Armenian Orthodox..."

When we arrived at the Church of the Nativity in Bethlehem I was surprised how run down the place looked. Elderly men sat around on stools wearing traditional long brown robes and sandals. They watched as we approached the church but said nothing to us. We were able to walk about inside, and a nun led us down a small flight of stairs into a room so small we had to duck our heads and enter just one at a time. This was the birthplace of Jesus. Because of the blockade we were the only visitors, and it made us all nervous knowing that we were not safe. We had been told of visitors being beaten up or knifed to death. It did sit uneasily at the back of my mind, so I was relieved when we finished our visit and returned to the Jewish part of Israel.

Although Jerusalem was the highlight of our visit to Israel there were many other places of great interest. In contrast to the Old City, Tel Aviv was a modern city full of young people sitting at outdoor cafes or lying on the beaches enjoying the sunshine.

What was surprising to me was the number of recent immigrants to Israel. There were wealthy Jews from New York City who had given up their high standard of living to move permanently to Israel where they had to learn to speak Hebrew, to live in modest apartments and where violence could erupt at any time. In contrast to them were the immigrants who had recently arrived from Eastern Europe.

As we walked about the streets in Tel Aviv we heard classical music at one corner and folk music at another. No matter where we went there was music of some kind that might be cheerful and carefree, but, more often, was sober and moody. When we arrived at the source, it would be a man playing a violin with such intensity that he looked to be transported into another world. On another street there would be a man playing a rhythmic folk song on an accordion. He, too, would appear to be gazing into the sky, not looking at the people who had stopped to listen to him. When we asked about the musicians, we learned that they were recent immigrants from Soviet bloc countries, who had come to Israel for freedom from the oppression under which they had been living. Many of them had been distinguished musicians in their own country but could find no work here.

The summer seminar was filled with lectures on Israeli history, meetings with scholars and authors and travel throughout the country. We went north to the Golan Heights to view a large area of land that Israel had annexed from Syria after the 1967 War. We learned that although the land appeared to be of little value, it was, in fact, extremely important because it provided thirty percent of Israel's water supply. We traveled to many parts of the country stopping to look at an expanse of land with no apparent value to discover that, in fact, it was vital to the country's well being. Once we stopped in the middle of the desert and over the brow of a small hill were led to a stairwell down which we climbed to discover a large aquifer in a natural looking cave where the cool air was a relief from the desert sun. Soon after leaving the aquifer, we came to a farm filled with flowers, able to flourish due to the underground water supply aided by special agricultural techniques developed by the Israelis. I was impressed at the ingenuity of these people. Much of the country was still desert, but slowly over the years the Jewish people had learned how to make the most of the land. They planted trees to develop small forests, and even gave us each a small tree to plant.

Before leaving Jerusalem, we had to see Yad Vashem, the monument dedicated to the six million Jewish victims of the Holocaust. It was one of the most moving places we visited. An eternal light stood in front of a vault holding the ashes of those who died and were brought to Israel. In one room the names of the victims were broadcast continuously twenty-four hours a day.

We visited the Sea of Galilee where Jesus carried out much of his mission, and we also visited the River Jordan. Both Biblical places were surprisingly small, particularly the river. So much has been written about the famous river I expected to see a substantial course of water, but it was only knee deep and barely flowed. At the time of our visit there were people being baptized, so we simply viewed the river from a distance.

Heading south, we stopped at the Dead Sea and floated in the salty water. We took mud baths that were supposed to rejuvenate us, and, while it felt good to splash around in the mud, after I had put a mud pack on my face and rinsed it off, my face looked just as it had earlier: the wrinkles and worry lines were still there.

One morning, a few of us hardy souls got up early to hike through the rocky canyons of the escarpment high above the Dead Sea. While we were in the area we also visited the Masada. I had never heard of the place before visiting Israel, but found it to be fascinating. The term zealot, came from the name given to a group of Jewish people who took refuge on the top of a rocky pinnacle in hopes of holding out against the Romans who, in the year A.D.66, were in control of the land. The Romans had killed most of the Jews who lived in the area except for this small band of zealots who vowed to defy the enemy by camping out on top of this huge rock sticking up from the Judean plateau. It was called the Masada, and had once been inhabited by ancient peoples. The zealots succeeded in settling on the rock by climbing a narrow earthen bridge, which was the only means of access to the top. Once they were settled in, they blocked the bridge and with sheer drop-offs on all the other sides of the rock, were able to live there for several years. The ancient peoples had carved passages and rooms and even an aquifer so that the zealots had plenty of water. Unfortunately, there came a time when their food supplies ran out. By that time, the Romans had encircled the rock cutting off any possible means of escape. The zealots decided to commit suicide rather than let the Romans capture them and force them into slavery.

There were so many sad aspects to Israel's history and yet the people we met remained upbeat despite the assaults from neighboring countries. In those days it seem as if every country that bordered Israel tried to make life miserable for these brave and industrious Jewish people. Traveling about the country it was easy to see proof of how diligent the people were and how dedicated they were to creating a country out of sand. Sadly, times have change as have the leaders of the country. Now, it appears that Israel has become aggressive towards its neighbors, Lebanon and Palestine. A new generation of Jewish people are looking at their place in the world and taking action. Whether that is a good thing or not is yet to be seen.

Dare To Do It!

The famous Wailing Wall in the Old City of Jerusalem.

The epic movie of 1993, *Schindler's List*, was about Oskar Schindler, a man who helped many survive during WWII. People put rocks on his grave as a sign of respect.

Professional musicians coming to Israel are often unable to find work.

Demonstrations by settlers, Israel, 1994.

Dare To Do It!

The Jordan River, Israel.

Nancy at the Dead Sea.

Dare To Do It!

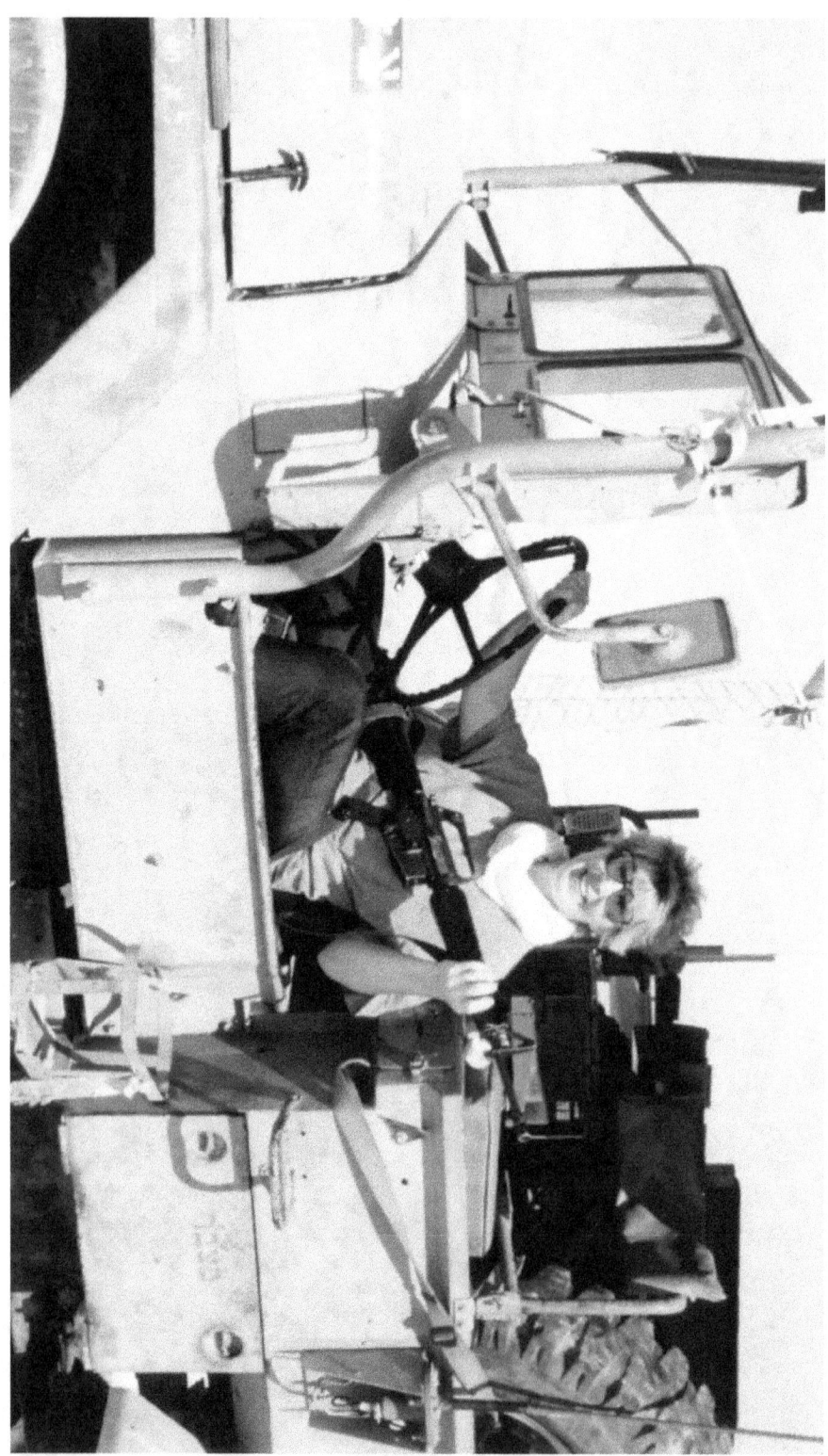

Nancy with gun, Israel, 1994.

Nancy Rubesch

EGYPT

Visiting Egypt was an exciting experience since it was a chance to see all those fascinating aspects of its ancient culture that intrigued me as a child: the pharaohs, the temples, the tombs and the writing system. Before our group was able to observe any of these, we were introduced to modern Egypt, a Muslim nation with decidedly different views than in Western countries.

We arrived in Cairo, the largest city in Egypt and were taken to the Shepheard Hotel. This hotel had been used as the setting for numerous movies because of its old world charm. We found the hotel pleasing although a bit stuffy and quiet. But that didn't last long. One night as we were heading to bed we heard this enormous noise coming from the floor above us. When we climbed the stairs and opened the door to the hallway, we discovered a group of children playing. One boy was riding a bicycle up and down, while other boys were bouncing balls against the walls to see how far of a zigzag pattern they could make. One boy was on roller skates and a group of older boys were rough housing, pushing each other around and then running up and down. We could see that the boys would not hear us if we asked them to quiet down, but after going to the concierge on the main floor we learned that the boys were allowed to make all the noise they wanted and management was not going to stop them. The reason for this was that the boys belonged to a Saudi Arabian family, who had rented out the entire floor and wanted their boys to have as much freedom as possible. Apparently, the Saudi family did not care if the noise disturbed other hotel patrons. The next morning when I went down to the breakfast buffet, there were several young women wearing the traditional black burkas, but they had the robes open and the headgear thrown back over their shoulders. They were comparing their clothing and jewelry to each other. All of them were wearing expensive looking dresses and designer high heels, gold necklaces, earrings and bracelets and heavy face makeup. The burka clearly covered them up when they were outside, but they seemed delighted in showing off their fancy clothing inside the hotel. Here was clearly a family who wanted people to know that they were wealthy. Interestingly, the evening before, I had noticed a couple of Saudi men sitting in the hotel bar. I could only conclude that when they were away from home they didn't worry about following the dictates of their religion.

The hotel incident was my introduction to a completely different culture, one that was difficult to comprehend. When our group was on our way to visit a university professor to discuss Israeli-Arab issues, we passed a crowd of people gathered in one of the city squares where a young woman from America was giving a speech. That evening back at our hotel while watching the news on the television, we saw the same square and the woman who had been speaking. The announcer discussed how this young woman, who had come from an Egyptian tribal family, had gone to America and made lots of money and now she had come back to Egypt where she was planning to build a center for impoverished youth. The announcer went on to discuss her accomplishments and how she had overcome many obstacles before she was successful. We were impressed.

The next morning, at breakfast, the front page of the local newspaper carried pictures of the very same young woman, describing her success in America and her plans. But, shockingly, the main focus of the article was on her death. She had been killed by her brothers because the father had decided she had brought shame and dishonor on the family because she had stood before the world wearing clothes that were deemed inappropriate. Apparently, honor killings were quite common and tolerated. It was so incomprehensible and sad. Just a few weeks before coming to Egypt there had been a beheading in Syria when two young people, who had run away and married, were captured, returned home and publically killed.

I encountered other incidents that were difficult to understand as an American living in a society where citizens took for granted their many freedoms. How lucky we were to live in a country without these strict cultural beliefs. I heard many Egyptian men and women who believed that people in America, particularly women, had loose morals. Here I was confronted again with different perspectives about social mores. It was one thing to read these divergent viewpoints in news magazines and another to be in the country hearing people tell me face to face that I lived in a decadent society. I had never looked at America as decadent. It was certainly an eye-opener.

We visited a school where the woman principal told of how lucky she was to be able to work, but that was only possible because her husband gave her permission and her son drove her to and from work each day. She was not allowed to ride in public transportation or drive a car on her own. This woman was in her sixties!

One time our group met with a professor who was a very strict Muslim. We sat around a small table, just fifteen of us and the professor. As I listened to this man speak I felt more and more uncomfortable, and if I could have gotten up and left without being obvious I would have. He spent an hour describing Americans as loose, immoral depraved souls. He went on to say that, given the chance, he would gladly kill every American he encountered. I don't know if this man was trying to shock us just for the hell of it, or if he was sincere. He certainly talked as if he meant every word. I was dumbfounded. How could anyone hate America? This man had never been there and yet he had already made up his mind. I came away from that lecture feeling very shaken. This meeting took place in 1994 long before the events that rocked the country later on. I had to admit that I was scared. How many other Muslims felt the same way?

We often visited educators and government officials in their offices. These people generally talked more about the problems that their own country had to solve rather than attacking Americans. To get to their offices was an adventure in itself. The city was very old, and its buildings appeared to be falling apart. Pieces from the façade of buildings would be lying on the sidewalk; stairwells were filthy and filled with trash; and elevators never worked. But once we arrived at an office, the interior would be immaculate. Apparently, people felt that only their immediate space needed to be cared for, and public places were ignored.

On a more cheerful note, we did visit the Cairo Museum. It, too, looked dusty and dirty and neglected throughout. But the King Tut exhibit, with each artifact encased in glass, was a fabulous collection of gold objects, especially the death mask. King Tut had been buried in three coffins: one wood, one with inlaid gold and one of solid gold. It must have been an amazing sight for Howard Carter, the archeologist, who first discovered the tomb and found it intact, since most of the tombs of the pharaohs had been plundered by robbers.

Upstairs in the one room that was completely clean and temperature controlled were the mummies. The mummy of Ramses II was the most exciting one in the room. The details on his face are so defined that it looked as if he could turn his head and open his eyes and speak. Most mummies were covered in some kind of wrapping, so to see this famous Egyptian king as he might look if he were sleeping was a very moving experience. History that can sometimes seem so dull was alive and well here in the Egyptian museum.

Before leaving Cairo, our group was taken to the Giza Plateau to see the pyramids. Looking in one direction, the pyramids appeared to be located in a vast desert, but looking in the opposite direction, the pyramids were fronted by apartment buildings and highways. It made sense that over the years urban development would eventually reach the Giza Plateau, but photographers always showed the pyramids framed against the desert. The reality took a bit of adjustment.

Dare To Do It!

The exciting thing about the pyramids was that if we didn't mind walking hunched over for fifteen to thirty minutes, we could enter the Great Pyramid of Khufu. The passageway was very narrow, dark and claustrophobic. The walk required everyone to move single file at a painfully slow pace. As soon as we had been plodding downward for several minutes, I felt as if the air was enveloping me in a stale miasma. I wanted to get out of there immediately, but when I stopped for a couple of seconds the people behind me began pushing me forward. I began silently telling myself to keep calm, but I could feel perspiration forming on my forehead and even running down my cheeks. Just when I thought I could no longer contain my panic, the passage opened up into a room about the size of a large living room. It was completely bare. Elaborate carvings, colorful murals and statues of royalty were always the focus of *National Geographic* photographs of Egyptian tombs, yet this funerary structure was devoid of all ornamentation. It was a bit of a downer, particularly since I still had to climb back up the passageway at the speed of a snail behind other people who had arrived and were probably just as disappointed, as they plodded upward in order to reach the outside.

There had been so many films, movies and articles devoted to these Wonders of the Ancient World, that I had completely romanticized them. I had planned to climb one of these unique structures, but when I stood next to the base of the Great Pyramid, I discovered the blocks that make up the pyramid were so huge that I could not reach to the top of the very first one. I could not physically climb the structure. But even if I could have been capable, it was against the law and a security guard quickly was at my side asking me to move back away from the pyramid. As a consolation "prize," I did have the opportunity to sit on a camel and have my picture taken. After my unusual camel ride in Australia I just wasn't all that interested.

After our usual morning meetings and lectures, we often had some free time. Some of the people in our group took naps, but a few of us went out to explore the city. That meant going repeatedly to the Khan al-Khalili Bazaar. This warren of narrow alleyways was so vast, that one visit did not provide enough time to see all the shops that sold gold, silver, leather, copper, brass and plenty of souvenirs. I had to purchase cartouches for each of my three children, with their names engraved in hieroglyphics. Besides the hieroglyphs, papyrus paintings were popular souvenirs so I purchased several of them to give to relatives.

After Cairo, our group flew to Luxor, the ancient city of Thebes. It was here that the various kings built most of their temples for the purpose of glorifying themselves and their accomplishments.

We visited two massive temples, Luxor and Karnak, both with walls and columns that dwarfed us humans, making us feel like insignificant Lilliputians next to the great pharaohs' gigantic structures. These monuments were clearly built to emphasize the importance of the ruler and to intimidate the common man. Every wall, column and obelisk was covered in carvings depicting the glories of the current king. When a new ruler became pharaoh, he would have the carvings altered or scratched out so that the only his deeds were evident. This was early political rhetoric! I loved walking through the ancient ruins wondering how these ancient people were able to erect structures so incredibly tall and still sturdy after thousands of years.

We crossed the Nile and headed for the Valley of the Kings where so many pharaohs were buried. I remember, as a kid, reading that scientists found most of the graves ransacked, but that King Tut's tomb had a mysterious curse that had resulted in several deaths to those who had disturbed it. Whether the curse had any validity or not, scientists removed the artifacts, so the only object of interest inside the tomb was King Tut himself. Having looked at detailed diagrams and photos of the murals inside the King's tomb, thanks to *National Geographic Magazine*, I was eagerly looking forward to seeing the young boy king.

The Valley of the Kings turned out to be a narrow piece of land surrounded on three sides by brown dirt-encrusted hills. Nothing on the surface would suggest the riches below. Several areas had been marked off with small numbered signs but, otherwise, there was no way to tell the kingly tombs from each other. A guide materialized spewing out statistics that were difficult to understand while we were trudging uphill in a pocket of air so hot that whenever I breathed my mouth became a furnace burning my tongue and making my eyes water. Perspiration ran down my back, my arms and even my legs. It was a hellish place to be, but, of course, worth every miserable step, as we approached King Tut's tomb. But then the unthinkable happened. The guide stopped, and while pointing at a number as proof we were at the tomb, continued to lecture us on all the marvelous discoveries in the Valley. The one thing he didn't do, was to invite us to step past the roped off entrance and go down into the burial chamber. In fact, none of the tombs were open to the public. What a major disappointment. It was hard to justify why we had come to this god-forsaken place. There was nothing to see, just barren hillsides devoid of even the tiniest piece of vegetation.

We trudged back to our vehicle and traveled past the Valley of the Kings stopping at another colossal architectural wonder, the Mortuary Temple of

Hatshepsut. I had never heard of this queen, but she was an important one as the massive temple dedicated to her clearly indicated. It was another building of gigantic proportions. Just the walk from the entrance to the actual temple was a challenge because of the heat. This temple was just as impressive as the others although it did not have as many hieroglyphs on all the columns that the kings had carved on their monuments. As we walked through the ancient structure I couldn't help but think of Cleopatra, the most well known female ruler of Egypt. She lived at a much later date and became famous in part due to her relationship with Mark Anthony. Her tomb had yet to be located. After learning more about Hatshepsut and her accomplishments I wonder why no one has made a film about her life. As I wondered, I wandered and finally headed back to the Nile where our group was scheduled to take a cruise from Luxor to Aswan.

After boarding our boat we sailed to Edfu and then on to Kom Ombo where there was a temple dedicated to Sobek, the crocodile god and the falcon god, Horus. The temple ruins were not as impressive as the ones at Luxor, but there were live crocodiles in a cage at which we could gape. All I could think was that the poor creatures were in enclosed spaces so small that they could not move about with no vegetation and the hot sun beating down on them. Apparently there are no animal rights organizations here. I found it quite depressing.

At Aswan we stayed at the Old Cataract Hotel, a lovely nineteenth century Victorian palace where Agatha Christie had once lived while she was writing one of her novels. Here we were given some time to relax, take a felucca ride on the Nile and visit the Agha Khan Mausoleum on top of the hillside across from the hotel. After a leisurely day we set off, flying to Abu Simbel, one of the most magnificent temples of them all.

The Great Temple of Ramses II at Abu Simbel had been built at the base of a cliff, but when the Aswan Dam was completed the lake that formed behind was expected to flood the area and cover the temple in hundreds of feet of water. UNESCO sponsored a project to save the temple by having it cut into pieces, hauled some two hundred feet to the top of the cliff and re-assembled. It took four years, and was a Herculean effort, but the results were well worth it. Many other temples were left buried in water, some even visible from the surface.

Abu Simbel was over 3,200 years old and was fronted by four seated sandstone statues of Ramses, each seventy feet high. Just as with the other temples built by Ramses, this one was even more magnificent in size and dwarfed us human beings. The temple was mathematically situated so that the sun's rays would stream through the structure lighting up the sculptures in the back of the temple on October 21 and February 21. It is thought that these days represented his birthday or some other major event in his life, but no one knows for sure.

After Abu Simbel, we flew back to Cairo for a farewell dinner and then departed for our homes. The seminar had been another incredible experience introducing me to two cultures, Israel and Egypt where the belief systems were clearly different from my American values. Visiting these two countries left me confused. Everyone in America takes for granted that the United States is the greatest country in the world. I still believe that. But now I had to accept the fact that there are people in the world who have negative opinions about America.

Many years later Jim and I and our family visited Egypt again and found the ancient ruins just as timelessly interesting as when I first visited. We were lucky to see Cairo while it was still safe. Unfortunately, in recent years radical religious groups have changed the country into an even more conservative society than when I visited in 1994. It appears to be no longer a safe place for tourists and this is sad given the ancient ruins in Cairo and in Upper Egypt along the Nile. One can only hope that the country will stabilize and offer safe travels for those visitors interested in ancient Egyptian history.

The pyramids outside of Cairo.

Only men smoke in cafés like this one in Luxor

The Temple of Edfu is an example of the architecture the Egyptians built along the Nile River.

The faluccas are common sights on the Nile.

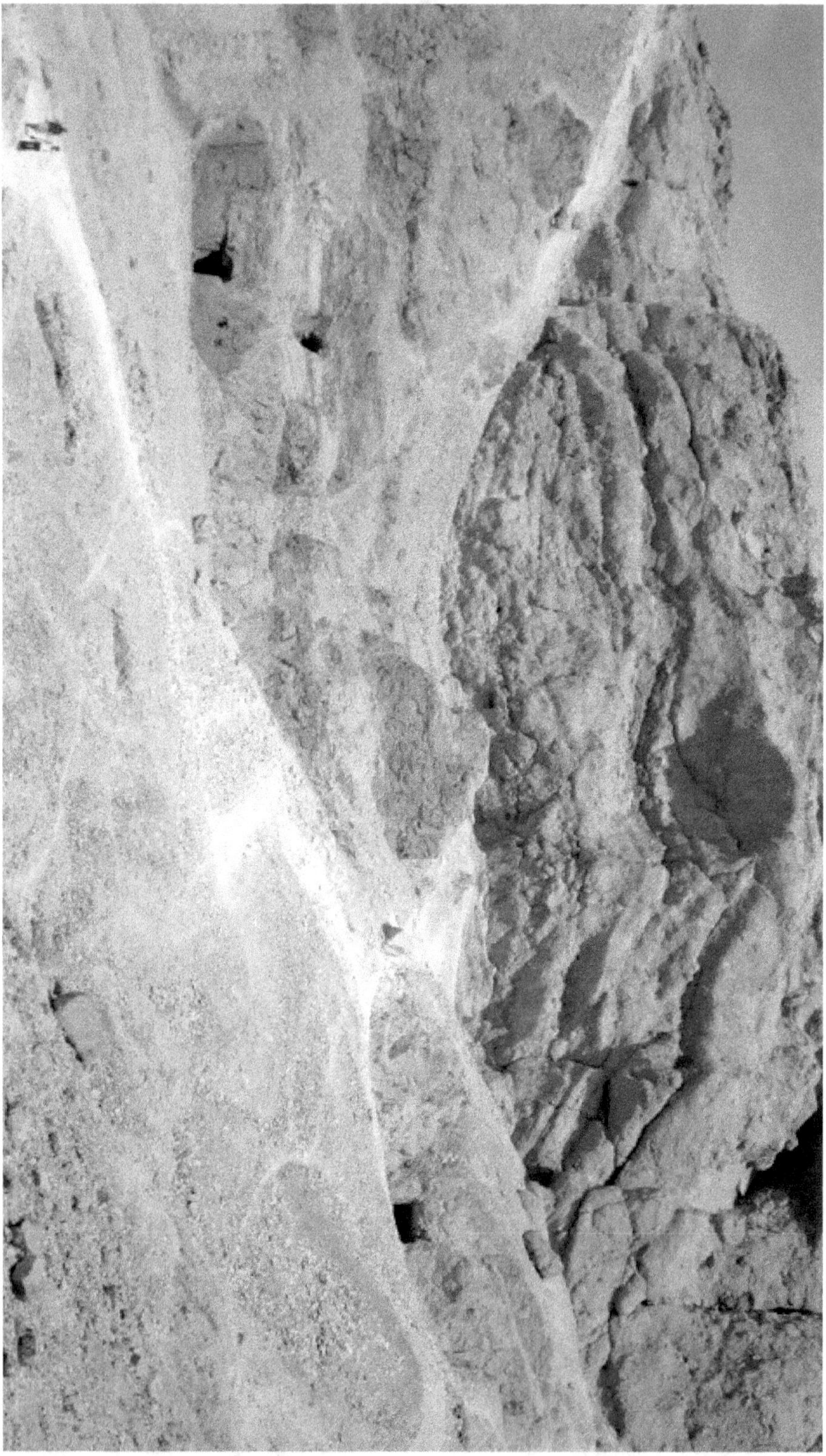

Dare To Do It!

This desolate valley hides the burial chambers.

Nancy Rubesch

MORE ADVENTURE

After participating in the government seminar to Egypt, opportunities to travel through teaching appeared to have dried up. Jim had retired, and so, I quit my position at the high school to become an educational consultant. By this time our three children had graduated from college, had married and were busy pursuing their chosen careers. They all lived in different parts of the world, giving Jim and I great excuses to visit them. Thus, for the next twenty years we traveled. Never in my wildest dreams would I have predicted that I would be able to continue visiting so many places, and, best of all, Jim came along to share the adventures. My full time job could be executed entirely on a computer making it possible for me to continue to work and travel at the same time. Life kept getting more interesting with every passing year.

There were so many trips to so many places that I can only describe some of the more unique adventures. Our oldest son had moved to Southeast Asia, so we spent many years exploring all of the countries in that area of the world. Our daughter went to Japan where her job sent her to many different locations in the country. Jim and I visited her wherever she happened to be living and fell in love with the people and their culture. When she moved to London, we often visited her there or met her in Paris and then headed to Greece where we would spend a couple months during the winter. Our youngest son and his wife went to South America for an extended stay, so Jim and I met up with them in Rio de Janeiro after exploring other parts of the continent. All these trips rewarded us with years of fantastic memories. Every day I gave thanks for my ongoing opportunities to travel.

Thailand

Our visits to see family began the year we flew to Thailand to see our oldest son, who had moved there after college. It turned into a grand adventure since Southeast Asia and Bangkok, in particular, were like no other places that we had been to. I remember the sun glittering off the rooftops of the many temples, stupas and unique structures in the Grand Palace, all of them visible from the Chao Phraya River that runs through the heart of the city. Besides taking us to several tourists sites, our son arranged for us to visit a beach resort in the Gulf of Thailand. The resort was incredibly picturesque with tidy whitewashed cottages scattered about a hillside overlooking the ocean. It was a refreshing change from the intense heat of the city, and it was blissfully quiet. My only concern was that I would be expected to wear shorts or a bathing suit, and I had a serious looking skin problem.

Before we left home I had scrutinized myself in the mirror and had decided that I needed to visit a local tanning salon to give my skin some color. I did not believe in baking in the sun or lying under ultraviolet lights, but I was desperate. I rationalized that a one-time zap of those nasty rays would not be deleterious and would, instead, turn me into a bronze goddess. Just as a plucked chicken turns brown with roasting, I, too, would be transformed by baking in one of those tanning booths. When I expressed my concerns about using one of the tanning beds, the salon attendant suggested that I opt for a spray-on tan instead. I merely had to stand in a booth while a machine covered my body with a product that would give me an all over healthy look. It would last for weeks and then fade away. It appeared to be the perfect solution. I paid for the paint job, stripped off my clothes, putting on tiny goggles to protect my eyes, and entered a booth. After standing motionless in one direction and then another the spray worked its way up and down my body. It was so simple I remember thinking that I would have to do this more often.

I left the paint booth, rinsed off, and, as I was toweling myself, happened to look in the mirror. Something was wrong. I moved closer and peered this way and that and to my horror saw that my skin was mottled with blotches that ranged from sickly yellow to bright orange. I looked as if I had a serious communicable disease. I must have screamed because the lady working at the salon came running into the change room, and when she saw me, she stopped with her mouth agape. Clearly, the spray-tan machine had malfunctioned. She was apologetic and offered me coupons for future use of the tanning facilities. Did she really think I would return after that fiasco? I went home and scrubbed my body over and over until the artificial tan began to fade. By the time Jim and I left Seattle for Bangkok my skin was still multi-colored but had changed to a less intense hue. While we moved about Bangkok I was conscious of my discolored skin, but no one else seemed to notice. By the time we flew to the island resort I probably was the only person who could see the patches of painted-on tan, looking much like faded mustard and ketchup swirled together in a random pattern that one might call abstract art.

Our oldest son fell in love with a beautiful Thai woman, married her and began raising a family. After our first visit, Jim and I started making trips every couple of years to see our two grand daughters grow from tiny tots to teens. Each time we arrived, our son and his wife had a trip planned to take us to different parts of the country. They also arranged trips so that we could visit Myanmar, Cambodia, Laos and southern China.

A temple set on the Chao Phraya River in Bangkok.

Golden temples can be seen throughout Thailand.

Thai dancers in their elaborate costumes.

Visiting the longneck women in Myanmar.

Penang

When his two daughters were preteens, our son sent them to boarding school in Mussoorie, India. On one of his visits Jim and I went along. We were impressed with the town, a former British hill station sitting atop a ridge in the foothills of the Himalayas with spectacular views of the mountains on one side and the northern plains on the other. It was an incredibly beautiful place with one drawback. In order to reach the town we had to take a taxi up a winding two-lane road that had been carved out of the side of the mountain so that a rocky wall was on one side and sheer drop-offs on the other. Our driver seemed to be racing the other cars to see if he could get to the next turn first. He passed on the shoulder while we closed our eyes and held our breaths as the vehicle careened ever so close to the cliff edge. After that experience I spent the next year worrying about the girls having to ride that road every time they had a vacation. Fortunately, they completed the year in Mussoorie without any accidents.

One year the youngest grand daughter transferred from Mussoorie to George Town in Penang, Malaysia. Jim and I accompanied our son and his wife on a trip there to see her how she was doing. We spent a week exploring the city and its colonial architecture. It was another fascinating discovery of a world so different from what we were used to in America. Many of the shopkeepers were Chinese so we often heard Chinese spoken on the street. Our grand daughter had been studying the Chinese language so her purpose in going to school there was to improve her conversational skills. Jim and I loved wandering about the old sections of town, but our most memorable experience was going to a nearby park where we encountered monkeys. Most people think of monkeys as cute and playful, but the monkeys that met us in the parking area and throughout the park were not only aggressive but also clever. Any person walking alone was fair game. The monkeys would encircle the visitor and then attack all at once. The only way to avoid this was to carry a large tree branch, and when the monkeys began to gather, swing the "bat" and run.

Old world colonial and Asian cultural influences in George Town, Penang.

These snakes live in the forests on Penang Hill.

Bali

Our trips to Thailand were always filled with interesting destinations so that every year Jim and I looked forward to our visits with our son and his family. But one year, instead of going to Thailand, our son suggested we meet in Bali, Indonesia. When we landed in Denpasar, the capital of Bali, we were a bit disappointed. It looked run down. The streets were full of souvenir shops and pleasure palaces to accommodate the droves of young people, who came to drink and party on holiday. After collecting our luggage we found a taxi to take us to Ubud, a small village set high in the mountains far from the coast and the capital.

Ubud, Bali was one of the most surreal and beautiful places on earth. Tropical plants and vines whose colorful flowers dangled profusely from tree branches framed emerald green rice fields. The terraced fields stood in uniform contrast to the wild, unkempt, forested areas. Along the lanes women walked like ballerinas gliding forth smoothly and effortlessly even while they had huge baskets balanced on their heads. The harmonious beauty of the land was so perfect that Ubud has often been called paradise on earth. Its aesthetic appeal attracted artists of all kinds, so that along the road approaching Ubud we saw many small workshops for silversmiths, wood carvers and batik artists. It was a place that seduced the visitor and made one feel as if he or she were living in a world apart from reality. As it turned out, our daughter, her husband and our youngest son and his wife joined us. It was a pleasure having the entire family together exploring the surrounding countryside and simply enjoying the ambiance of the tropical setting. Soon the week had passed and it was time for our children to return to their respective homes and careers. I can't recall any place on earth that Jim and I found so difficult to leave. We even talked about staying another week by ourselves, but, as it turned out, a unique adventure beckoned.

No sooner had family members departed, when Jim announced: "We need to go to Komodo Dragon Island." At first I thought he was out of his mind. He wanted to go to a remote island where prehistoric creatures wandered freely about? He had clearly been out in the sun too long. I was happy just exploring the nearby island of Lombok where we were able to hire a guy to take us out snorkeling. That was my idea of adventure – tropical fish, a boat ride and, most importantly, being close to civilization. To go to a primitive island to see huge monstrous lizards was certainly an over-the-top adventure. Since those dragons had been featured on *Animal Planet* or some similar television program, there were probably other people, like Jim, who wanted to visit the island. Thus, I reasoned, someone would have built a hotel and restaurant to accommodate those tourists. I agreed that the island was bound to be a great adventure, but I wasn't enthusiastic. Little did either of us know what we were headed for.

We left Bali and ferried over to the neighboring island of Lombok. After riding a local bus to the eastern side of the island, we boarded another ferry to take us to the island of Sambawa. Sambawa was very rural and remote with thatched roofed farms poking out from the tropical vegetation. The lush green landscape was exceptionally beautiful, and I never got tired of looking at it even though we were on the local bus for over eight hours. When we finally arrived in Bima, a small village on the eastern coast of Sambawa, we were just in time to board the ferry that plied the waters between Sambawa and Flores, the next island to the east.

The ferry must have been waiting for the bus because as soon as everyone from the bus had boarded, it left the pier and headed out into a very choppy sea. The straits between the two islands were well known for being treacherous, and the heaving waves certainly were proof of that. We rode for about an hour when the ferry stopped and sat with its motor idling. We tossed and turned, and it felt as if the ferry was going to be smashed to pieces by the chaotic waves. Finally, a small motorboat appeared on the horizon and soon approached us. This was our transportation to Komodo Dragon Island.

The rough jerky motion of the water forced the small motor launch to stop some distance away. The ferry crew motioned for us to climb down the ladder and jump into the small boat. I hesitated as the gap between the ferry and boat was alarmingly wide. Suddenly, I was pushed from behind. It was clear that the ferry personnel had no time for timid tourists. The next thing I knew, as I crawled down the ladder on the side of the ferry, someone grabbed my arm and flung me into the small boat. I hit the deck on my knees and would have cried out in pain if I were not so relieved to be safely settled in the boat. Jim was able to bridge the gap with no problem, and after a couple of more dexterous young people made the jump look effortless, we headed toward Komodo Island. Some thirty minutes later we saw a green blotch on the horizon, our destination.

When we arrived at the pier, a park ranger greeted us and led us to an open-air pavilion outfitted with tables and benches where we were told we could purchase a simple meal later that evening. The ranger said he would take us on a trek into the jungle to see the komodo dragons as soon as we were ready. We stowed our backpacks in the corner of the building and went outside to meet our leader. While he fiddled with his shotgun, he told us about the dragons, how they lived, what they ate and how many people had died from the jaws of these fierce creatures. He emphasized the importance of us staying together, walking single file and not talking loudly. As we hiked through the dense forest on a well-worn path, the ranger stopped occasionally to point out dragon lairs. They looked like large hollowed-out holes in the ground and frankly were not all that exciting. Like the rest of the group, I was hoping one of those prehistoric animals would come charging out of the bushes in front of us. Instead, the hike was peaceful and quite ordinary.

Finally we came to an open area where there was a blind overlooking a small gully. We were herded inside the fenced-off area, and then the ranger told us he would summon the dragons. It sounded rather strange. Did he have the dragons trained to come on command? In fact, he did. He simply rang a bell, and then suddenly out of the woods in all directions came huge fierce monsters, some running at incredibly fast speeds. In the past a goat had been tied in the gully, but the pitiful cries from the goat and the bloody mess as the dragons tore the animal apart, had distressed many of the visitors. The bell now worked its Pavlovian magic allowing us all to see the animals in action up close and personal without the sound effects and gore. Watching those huge creatures moving with so much speed and agility made me realize that the dull hike to the blind was a blessing. Having one of those hungry creatures jump out of the bushes would have given me a heart attack. The spine tingling sensation observing those dragons intensified as we visitors hiked back out of the forest. No one wanted to be the last person in line.

The crazy thing was that once we returned to the pavilion we discovered a komodo dragon was lying directly under the steps that led up to the restaurant. We had to assume that the dragon was too old and too sated to desire one of us. Still, there was that uncertainty. What if it wanted an afternoon snack? No one lingered on the steps.

After our exciting encounter with those wild creatures the ranger left us at the pavilion reminding us to stay nearby and not stray into the forest alone. He recounted how dragons bite off a leg of its prey, depositing their poisonous saliva into the victim which weakens it to the point that it cannot run away. Then the dragon eats the animal alive. After his vivid description, he told us again about the handful of tourists who had been killed in just such a manner. With that happy note, he left, and Jim and I decided it was time for us to leave as well.

When we inquired about returning to Sambawa that late afternoon, we learned that the boat would not be returning until the next day. What a surprise! We had only one small daypack with a couple bottles of water and the clothes we were wearing: sandals, shorts and tee shirts. When we asked where we would be able to sleep, the ranger pointed to a plywood box tacked together clinging to the hillside above the pavilion. No problem, he said. We could sleep anywhere we wanted up there.

We hiked up the hillside and stepped into the structure. It was basically a rectangular box partitioned into compartments. Each "room" had one cutout for the doorway and one cutout for a window. In the middle of the box was a large jug holding water and next to it a hole. One used the "toilet" and then scooped water out of the jug to flush. The facilities were a little less than I had envisioned.

Even though we were wearing a minimal amount of clothing, the "room" was hot and the floor was hard. There was no bed, electricity or other civilized amenities. We glanced into one of the other compartments and saw that those visitors had set up a tent and had rolled out sleeping mats. Someone must have told them before coming to be prepared. We sat down in our compartment and talked about the hike we had just experienced. We both agreed that the trip to this remote island was well worth it to see the dragons in their own habitat.

When it began to get dark outside, we lay down on the wood floor cradling our heads in our arms. We tried rolling up the daypack, but it made a poor substitute for a pillow. The excitement of the day helped put us into a pleasant sleep…for a while. Suddenly, I woke as I felt tiny feet and a furry body run over my legs. Then, in quick order, I felt another creature and then another. I probably screamed as I pushed myself to a sitting position with my back against the wall. Jim, too, had awaken and sat up against the wall. We could hear scurrying noises as if a thousand creatures had evaded our room. When Jim turned on the small flashlight he kept in his pocket, we saw rats, their beady eyes staring at us. The room appeared to be completely full of rats the size of small cats. I am surprised I didn't have a heart attack right then and there. Jim stomped his feet a few times and the nasty creatures momentarily disappeared.

Shaken by the event, I decided to sit up the rest of the night with my back plastered to the wall. Jim just lay back down and was soon asleep. I shivered as I heard the scurrying of the rats running about elsewhere in the plywood box. Each time something moved I banged my water bottle on the floor to deter the rats from coming into our room. I must have dozed off for the next thing I knew I felt as if I were being smothered. Deep in the darkness before morning light, millions of beetles invaded our room. There were so many that I had to bury my head in my arms to make a hollow space where I could breathe. If I looked up for an instant the insects tried to invade my nose, ears and mouth. I tried to shrink into a fetal position to protect my body from the on slot, but the beetles swirled about stinging my skin wherever they banged into me. I don't know if the rats were still about since I didn't dare to look up, but I continued to bang the water bottle on the floor in hopes that they would stay away. Jim woke once in the night, turned on his flashlight, saw the beetles, turned the light off and went back to sleep. That had to be one of the longest nights I had ever experienced, and I could not fathom how Jim could sleep right through it.

In the morning we found orange beetles lying dead all over the floor. Outside our petition the entranceway and the toilet area were carpeted with beetles. To walk to the toilet or to leave the plywood box, Jim and I had to hold onto the petition walls to keep from slipping on the hard shells of the dead bodies.

We hiked down the hill to the pavilion, and, while having breakfast, we noticed that there were small animals running around on the rafters above us. They looked like rats, but the ranger told us that they were baby komodo dragons. At least the roof was high enough above us so that I didn't feel threatened by their presence, but I still cringed every time I saw a movement above us.

While waiting for the boat to arrive we noticed several deer standing or lying in the grass just outside. They all had one leg missing. It was a sad thing to see since we knew that the dragons would soon eat these beautiful creatures.

The motor launch arrived in the late morning, and we climbed aboard. The boat motored out into the choppy channel where the ferry was waiting for us. I was shoved from behind, and someone on the ferry grabbed my arm and dragged me forward until I could reach the ladder. I clamored up and into the ferry, while Jim easily bridged the gap between the launch and ferry with little effort. We safely returned to Sambawa, took the bus across the island, ferried to the next island and so on until we returned to Bali. We stayed one night in Denpasar and then took an international flight back to our home in the Pacific Northwest. Even with the horrific invasion of undesirable creatures in the night, Jim and I agreed that our adventure to Komodo Dragon Island was a mighty fine experience.

Women in Bali carry huge bundles on their heads.

People in Bali going to worship a one of the temples.

Komodo Dragon, Komodo Island, Indonesia.

Japan

When our daughter moved to Japan to live for many years, Jim and I took the opportunity to visit her on several occasions. On one of our visits, Jim and I decided to take the Shinkansen bullet train to Beppu, a famous hot springs resort town on Kyushu. We assured our daughter, who was working and could not accompany us, that we would not get lost when she voiced her concerns about the two of us traveling by ourselves. She had good reason to worry; we got into trouble from the start.

We went to the train station and after purchasing our tickets proceeded to the platform where we waited for our train. Peering down the track we saw a train arriving. Suddenly, a wind gust blasted across the platform hitting us so hard that we felt as if we were going to be lifted right off our feet. In less than a minute the train swooshed by and was gone. We must have looked confused for a Japanese woman came over to us. She shook her head, "no," at the place where we were standing and gestured for us to move back behind a red line painted on the platform. When we purchased our ticket, no one had mentioned that those fast trains could actually suck a person off the platform if he or she stood too close to the edge.

Knowing how precise the Japanese trains run, we were impressed when our train arrived two minutes early. We boarded and, as we were walking down the aisle to our reserved seats, the train took off, immediately gaining a high rate of speed. The ride was so smooth we had no trouble negotiating the center aisle to our assigned seats, but when we got there, two ladies were occupying them. We politely asked them to move, holding up our tickets so that they could see that they matched the seat numbers. One of the women pointed to our tickets and shook her head, 'no.'

People sitting nearby rapidly exchanged comments, which we did not understand since neither Jim nor I spoke Japanese. Our confused expressions prompted a man sitting several seats back, to come forward. While the people in the nearby seats were all talking at once, the man said in halting English, "Not your seats. Your seats on next train." When the man pointed out that train number on our tickets and showed us a train schedule, we discovered that, in fact, we were on the wrong train. Apparently there was another high-speed train just a couple minutes behind the one we were on.

Before we could properly thank the man, he had returned to his seat. Jim and I didn't know what to do. We moved to the end of the car and stood there for the rest of the trip. And when the conductor came by he looked at us, shook his head, and left us there. We knew Japanese trains were efficient, but we could hardly believe that two trains traveling at hundreds of miles per hour on the same track could be scheduled so close together. What if the one train was going slightly faster than the other, the other going slightly slower? The chance of a major crash seemed highly probable, and yet, the timing was so precise that Shinkansen bullet trains had never been in any accidents.

In no time we had zipped across the island of Kyushu and arrived in Beppu. The train station was centrally located so that we simply left the station and headed up a nearby hill where there were onsen businesses lining both sides of the street. We didn't know whether to visit the hot springs with the crocodile exhibit or the hot springs with the floral garden display. We finally picked one at random, paid the nominal entrance fee and walked down a hallway until we found a changing room.

No one was around to direct us, so we simply removed our clothing, stuffed everything in a locker and with the tiny towel the receptionist had handed us, we walked through a doorway into a large room that had rectangular pits lined up in rows. We assumed that the pits held different types of materials that were supposed to be beneficial to the skin. Since we could not read any of the identifying signs, we decided to be safe and lie down in the sand pits. At first, we sat and piled the sand over our legs and then our torsos. As we buried more of our bodies we had to lie down. I assume that at busier times an attendant would help cover customers, but more sand would have definitely made me feel claustrophobic. As it were, the sand cuddled around my body relaxing me and making me sleepy. I never realized that a sand box could be so beneficial.

After lying contently for a few minutes in the warm sand, Jim and I decided it was time to explore the rest of the onsen. We hosed ourselves off and walked through another door that led outside. There was a large pool of crystal clear water where steam rose from the surface, and an inquiring toe let us know that the water was very hot. Before we ventured into the deep soaking pool, we decided to try wading down a man-made channel that ran the length of the building from which we had emerged. It was only ankle deep but the bottom was composed of sharp stones so that walking on them was supposed to massage the bottom of the feet. I found it extremely painful and gave up after only advancing a couple of feet. Jim did likewise.

We decided to venture out into the pool until we could sit comfortably neck deep in the soothing mineral laden water. Once we were soaking and able to relax, I looked around and saw that there were three young men on the other side of the pool. They were yakking away and giggling, but we had no idea

Dare To Do It!

what they were saying and didn't pay much attention, until we were getting out of the pool and started back to the shower and changing room. One of the men called out to me in English, "Have a nice day. We enjoyed your visit since we don't normally see women in the men's section of the onsen." My first reaction was to hide behind my towel, but it was so small it was of no value at all. I was hot from soaking in the pool, but my face was even hotter from embarrassment. Jim thought it was funny. Later, when describing the experience to my daughter, she just laughed and said that I would never see those men again, so it was no big deal.

After visiting with our daughter in Kumamoto, the main town on Kyushu, Jim and I headed to Tokyo where we were to board our plane for America. We decided to spend a couple of days in the city exploring some of the areas we had missed on previous trips to Japan. Because even the least expensive hotels were beyond our budget, we booked a couple of beds in the dorm of a hostel. After climbing several flights of stairs we were surprised to find a huge room that was completely empty. There were closets at one end that held futons that we were expected to use, but otherwise the place was devoid of furniture. What surprised us was that there were no people.

Having a gymnasium-sized room to ourselves was just fine, but there was one slight drawback. The toilet and bathing facilities were on the floor below. That meant that to use them we had to put on our clothes and run down two flights of stairs and then run even faster, depending upon our needs, to the center of the building where there were two doors, each labeled in Japanese with the appropriate male or female character. We used the facilities that evening, but the next morning when I decided to take a shower, things took a strange turn.

I got up early that morning and ran downstairs carrying my change of clothing. I quickly went in, stripped off my nightshirt, piled everything in a locker and grabbed one of those postage stamp sized towels. I opened the door to the washing area where there was a row of low stools facing the water spigots. But just as I started to sit down on a stool, I saw a young man, completely naked washing himself. We both looked at each other with startled expressions, and then I turned and ran back to the changing room. I threw on my clothes, but before I got out the door, I checked the Japanese characters above the men and women toilets. The young man was in the woman's bath. I wanted to run back inside and tell him of his faux pas, but then who am I to comment when I had made a similar mistake just days before.

Famous temple in Tokyo.

Harajuku fashion in Tokyo.

Typical Japanese landscape.

Kumamoto Castle on Kyushu Island, Japan.

Entrance to an onsen (hot springs), Kyushu, Japan.

Dare To Do It!

France

When our daughter moved from Japan to London, Jim and I visited her there, or we met her in Paris. We loved the excuse to visit both cities, spending the days exploring and the evenings and weekends with our daughter going to art exhibits, street fairs and gourmet restaurants. I thought our urban explorations great adventures, especially when we found places off the beaten path away from the hordes of tourists.

On one such trip to Paris, we spent several days visiting with our daughter and then she had to go back to London to her job. Having more time to explore, Jim and I decided to travel to Annecy, France to see the small village that was reputed to be so picturesque. The setting of the village on the edge of a lake surrounded by mountains was just as charming as we had been told, but, unfortunately, the place was overwhelmed with tourists. It was only at night after the dozens of tour buses left that we enjoyed wandering about the streets. Once we had explored the town and ridden the bus to the far end of the lake and back, we were ready to head up into the mountains for a bird's eye view of the lovely setting.

Early one morning Jim and I left Annecy on a bus traveling to the top of a nearby mountain. The bus chugged slowly upward through heavy forests of evergreens until it rounded a bend and the road ended. Except for one small building and a parking lot, the entire summit was fenced off into pastureland with a few dirt roads between each area. Jim decided to relax on a bench near the building and enjoy the view of the Alps in the distance. I decided to hike down one of the roads to see where it went. Along the way I was overtaken by a couple of hikers who veered off into a narrow path that went up a hillside towards the edge of the mountain. I decided to follow them in hopes of being able to see Annecy and the lake from high above. Unfortunately the view was blocked by trees and the path turned steeper as I climbed. By the time I reached the top of the incline, the couple I had followed had disappeared. But the path was clearly worn so it was easy to follow.

A small number of cows had been munching grass nearby, but when they saw me, they decided to come over and investigate. They trod over the grass and onto the path in front of me. I didn't know what to do except stop and wait for them to get bored and leave. But suddenly out of the corner of my eye I saw a huge bull heading towards us. I looked around but the path was along side the pasture fence and on the other side was a drop off. Would the bull attack me? The cows clustered about just a few feet from me jostling about in disarray.

Suddenly, the bull climbed upon the back of one of the cows and began humping away. I wasn't sure what was louder, the bull panting or the cow screeching. I quickly turned around and scurried back down the path to the road.

When I arrived back at the parking lot, Jim suggested we walk down to the midway point where the bus had stopped on the way up the mountain. Since the sun was hot and there was no shade it seemed like a sensible plan. I started to head down the road, but Jim said he had a better idea. If we climbed the small hill behind the building, we could take a shortcut down through a meadow to the midway bus stop and it would be a bit cooler than walking a hot dusty road.

When we got to the top of the little hill behind the building, we could see the meadow and the buildings at the bottom of the steep hillside where the bus had stopped earlier on our trip upward. It appeared to be a great plan.

As soon as we started walking through the meadow we ran into difficulties. The lovely green-carpeted hillside looked smooth from a distance, but up close, the earth below the vegetation was uneven and full of potholes. Instead of a pleasant hike, we stumbled along tripping here and there and soon wondered if this plan should be aborted. But the hillside was so steep that we decided it would be better to continue on than to try to climb back up to the top. Initially, the distance from the top to the bottom of the hill looked relatively short, but the longer we stumbled downward the further away the buildings at the midway point seemed to be. Finally after an hour or more, we reached the bottom. We still had some hiking to do to reach the bus stop and the afternoon had quickly disappeared. If we missed the bus we would be stranded on the mountain.

Once we were on the relatively flat shelf where the buildings were situated, we realized that we were inside a pasture. The land was soggy and mucky the closer we got to the buildings. There were cows clustered in one area, but they had clearly made use of the entire pasture, as we had to dodge around huge cow patties the diameter of car wheels. The pungent smell was bad enough, but every time we passed a patty, swarms of flies suddenly filled the air around us. When we finally managed to get to the fence next to the road, Jim lay down on the ground and inched his way under the barbed wire. I wasn't about to get down in that awful muck when I could simple hold one barbed wire down and climb through. Just as grabbed the wire Jim yelled, but it was too late. Jolted with electricity I screamed and fell backward into the very muck I had tried to avoid. After I got my feeling back in my arm, I crawled over to the fence and lay down on my back. I remember looking to the side and realizing that my face was only an inch from a huge cow patty. Huge flies stared me in the eyes. I held my breath as I inched my body under the wire and onto the roadside. We managed to jog down the road arriving at the bus stop just in time to board for our trip back to Annecy. The aroma of cow pasture hung heavily over us causing several passengers to look at us in dismay as they quickly moved to seats some distance from us. Later, Jim and I both had to agree that this was definitely an adventure of a rather pungent kind.

Nancy Rubesch

French bovine.

Dare To Do It!

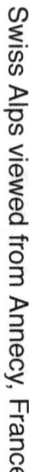

Swiss Alps viewed from Annecy, France.

South America

Our youngest son was happy to stay put in Seattle where he and his wife actively pursued many outdoor activities. But one year the two of them took a year's leave of absence from their respective jobs to spend six months in Australia and six months in South America. Having acquired a couple of airline tickets to fly wherever American Airlines went, Jim and I took it as a sign that we should try to meet up with them. We booked our itinerary, planning to fly to Argentina and explore Buenos Aires before heading to Rio de Janiero where our son and his wife were temporarily living.

Although we were only in Buenos Aires for a short time, my impression of this city, often called, "the Paris of South America," was of tree-lined avenues, clean streets and impeccably dressed people hurrying here and there. Besides the beauty of the environment, the thing that stood out the most was the beauty of the women. Every female we saw had perfect features, hair and bodies. We were told that the country had one of the highest rates of plastic surgery in the world. I felt rather dowdy walking amongst all those attractive women and, while I enjoyed the city immensely I was happy to move on.

When we arrived in Rio de Janeiro we fell in love with the beautiful setting. The mountains jutting up creating lovely bays fronted by golden sand beaches were picture-postcard lovely. Walking along the waterfront, we saw clusters of people on the beaches playing volleyball, running next to the water's edge and throwing Frisbees. It looked as if the residents of Rio knew how to enjoy life. I loved the fact that the women, no matter what size or shape, wore bikinis and clearly appeared happy with their bodies. We could identify with the laid back Brazilian ambiance.

While our main purpose of visiting Rio was to see our son and his wife, we also took advantage of the bus system along the beaches to see all the famous sights. We took the telephonic to the top of Corovado Mountain and then had to climb many stairs to finally arrive at the iconic statue, Christ the Redeemer. The views from the top were spectacular.

One night Jim and I, our son and his wife decided to attend a samba show. The dance event took place in a large auditorium clearly set up to perform for tourist groups. The different acts ranged from nearly nude women dancing to fast rhythmic songs to women dressed in such elaborate costumes they could barely move across the stage. The show was truly spectacular. Afterward I decided to have my picture taken with one of the showgirls. When we went back stage we were greeted by a young woman so heavily made-up her face looked drawn on with a heavy black marker. The thick lines around her eyes extend out across her temples in an exaggerated cartoonish look while her brows were painted in large arcs so far up her forehead as to almost touch her hairline, and her lips were drawn around her mouth so far from her natural feature as to be similar to a clown's face. Apparently the makeup had to be this heavy in order to be seen from a distance. With platform shoes, she loomed over us larger than life. Her body seemed to be encased in a body suit that was so tight around the waist that it looked as if she must have a difficult time breathing, much less dancing. My illusion of a beautiful showgirl had been shattered.

After the samba show we piled into a taxi and gave the driver the address of our hotel. As soon as we had climbed in and the door was shut, he took off at a very high speed. He careened around corners and flew through stop signs and red lights. We yelled at him to slow down or to stop, but he said he couldn't do that. Every time we went through an intersection I cringed, afraid we would either run into another vehicle or one would crash into us. When we finally got to our destination, we were all ready to bolt out of the cab, but the driver stopped us. He said that he realized we were scared, but he said that crime was so great at night that he didn't dare to stop at lights or intersections as gangs would materialize and beat and rob everyone. He said he was only trying to be sure that we were safe and that he was safe as well. Shaken and not knowing whether to believe the cab driver or not, we hurried up to our rooms. From our window we could look down of several lighted soccer fields where games were in progress. It looked so normal and civilized. Being skeptical, we asked the hotel personnel about the frightening ride back to the hotel, and the staff assured us that people stayed in at night because the crime rate was so high.

A couple dancing the tango in a neighborhood plaza, Buenos Aires.

There are many beaches in Rio, and all are lovely.

"Christ the Redeemer" statue being renovated, Rio de Janeiro.

Samba dancing events often end with the performers dressed in elaborate costumes.

Alaska

After spending a week exploring the city with our son and his wife, we had to return home. He and his wife continued their travels even hiking the Torres del Paine near the tip of South America. We were delighted to find our son so adventurous. He clearly took after his father, preferring to explore remote places rather than go to the more popular tourist centers found in urban areas.

Over the next several years, Jim and I traveled all over the world. In the winter we left for warmer climates and in the spring and summer we took trips into the wilderness of northern Alaska and Canada. One of our most memorable adventures occurred when we drove up the Alcan Highway to Alaska. Since we had only a pup tent, we stayed in commercial campgrounds because the one attempt to set up camp in a state park was thwarted by a moose and her offspring. We even found canoeing could be hazardous when a huge moose suddenly thrust its huge rack out of the water only a few feet from us. We frantically back paddled as far away as we could. We loved the state's untamed nature where people shared the land with wild animals on their doorsteps. Whether out in a forest or in the middle of town, locals love to tell about the bear or moose that had just wandered through town.

One day we decided to take a ride on a plane making a mail run to a small Eskimo village above the Arctic Circle. Little did we know when we purchased our ticket that we might end up stranded in a place so remote that there were no roads in or out of the area.

The small commercial airplane had about ten seats lined up on either side of the cabin. Several passengers were already seated when we boarded, and they appeared to be native Alaskans heading to Anatuvik, the small village that was our destination.

At first the flight was a pleasant experience as we cruised above the forested land. From the sky I saw an untamed wilderness that stretched as far as I could see. If the plane were to go down it did not look as if there would be any way to rescue survivors. But the plane engine sounded healthy and the ride was smooth. I tried to put such thoughts out of my mind.

Suddenly, the plane began shaking violently. The vibration was so intense I gripped the armrest with one hand and used the other to brace myself against the seat in front of me. I looked out the window. A mountain of jagged rock was so close that it looked as if the plane's wing would scrape its side, tearing off and sending us plunging into the depths below. Then, unexpectedly, the plane dropped several feet before regaining altitude. By this time the plane was flying sideways and shaking as if every nut and bolt would work itself loose causing the entire capsule to fall apart in midair. Stomach churning and head pounding, I looked about and was amazed to see the other passengers calming sitting in relaxed positions. Even the pilot looked unfazed, sitting with his feet on the dash while drinking a coke as if nothing unusual was happening. The violent movement of the plane was too intense for me to have imagined it. Finally spewed forth from the center of the mountain range, the plane righted itself and calmly flew on to its destination no thanks to the pilot.

We had just flown through the Brooks Range, one of the most remote places in Alaska. Shortly thereafter, I saw some grayish-brown buildings looking as if they were partly buried in the permafrost. We had finally arrived in Anatuvik. Once on the ground, the passengers filed off the plane and quickly disappeared. Jim and I got out of the plane to stretch our legs, and I remember how happy I was feeling the earth under my feet.

While we waited for the pilot to check in, Jim decided he needed to use the toilet and off he went to a nearby building. While he was gone, the pilot reappeared and after climbing into the cockpit began to rev the engine as if he were going to take off. I ran under the wing and yelled up to him to wait, and when he looked out he seemed surprised that I was there. He said there wasn't time to wait since he still had to fly back through the Brooks Range while the weather was good. We had to go back the way we came? I felt like throwing up. I climbed up on the wing just as he started to shut the door, but I pleaded with him to wait just a minute more. Finally, I saw Jim ambling toward us. I waved frantically gesturing to him to hurry. He broke into a run and reached the plane just as the pilot made it clear he wasn't waiting any longer. Before either of us could settle into a seat in the now empty plane, he shoved the plane into gear and we took off.

We flew through the Brooks Range again. I shall never forget that name, a synonym for hell. The return trip was just as miserable and frightening as it had been before. If this was adventure it sure was exhausting. Once we were back on the ground in Anchorage, I could feel the tension begin to leave my body. We headed to our pup tent for a much needed nap. Later, when we had recovered from our experience, we both agreed that it was a grand adventure.

Nancy Rubesch

Hiking in Alaska could mean an encounter with a bear.

Dare To Do It!

Canoeing in Alaska can be dangerous if a moose happens to be in the water.

The commuter plane that flies to Anaktuvuk Pass, Alaska.

Everyone commutes by plane in Alaska.

The Brooks Range is in a remote part of northern Alaska.

Dare To Do It!

Nancy Rubesch

ACROSS NORTH AMERICA

We continued to travel year after year until one day we realized we had entered our seventies and were about to celebrate our fiftieth wedding anniversary. Why not celebrate it by cycling across the U.S? We had traveled all over the world, but how much of our only country had we explored? We drove to many destinations in the United States, but encapsulated in a metal vehicle barreling down a freeway did not offer many opportunities to see America. To do so, we needed to slow down and take back roads where we could really explore the countryside, and what better way to do it than on a bicycle.

This bike trip was in many ways the greatest adventure of all. All our other travel depended upon some kind of motorized transportation, but on this adventure, we expected to complete four thousand miles under our own power. Both Jim and I agreed that we had to do the entire distance cycling or walking, if need be. It would take muscle power and persistence. We had the determination, but did we have the strength? Our friends and acquaintances were skeptical. They simply had us stereotyped as too old to sustain three to four months of daily cycling. But they clearly did not know us very well. We never had any doubts about succeeding. Perhaps that was because we had no clue as to what we were getting into.

We originally planned to cycle across the U. S., but after giving it some thought we decided that a better idea would be for us to pedal across the northern states from Washington to Michigan and then turn north going up the Saint Lawrence River to its mouth on the Gaspe Peninsula. When our children were very young Jim and I had made just such a trip, but we traveled by car. We had fond memories of our early adventure and always wanted to repeat it. However, we never thought we would return on bicycles.

In addition to celebrating our fifty years of marriage we felt the trip would also be a reinforcement of our commitment to staying fit and healthy. We hoped that we would celebrate our sixtieth anniversary on a similar bike trip, but we also recognized that as we aged we just might find the challenge too much.

The first question that came to mind was why would anyone want to spend four months cycling across America when one could drive the distance in a week in comfort? My husband, Jim and I envisioned bonding with nature on quiet country roads, enjoying picturesque pastures and farms, blue skies and sunshine. The reality turned out to be quite different. We simply had not thought about spending day after day coping with traffic or struggling up mountains while searing pain in our legs over shadowed that of sitting on a bike seat all day long. People always mention how miserable a bike ride must be perched on that tiny seat. And, in fact, it was not comfortable. That hard triangle of leather poked and prodded one of the most sensitive parts of the body. How could anyone find that enjoyable? But after an hour of cycling, muscles in the arms, legs and neck that have never spoken before, would be suddenly screaming. A pain in the behind was nothing compared to the discovery of muscles we never even knew we had that were yelling at us in strident protest.

We were not hard-core bikers. The regulars at the gym certainly gave us doubtful looks when we said we were biking across the continent. We didn't look like the guy in the skin-tight jersey showing off his muscles or the gal in the sports bra flaunting her tiny bare waist. Our antique sagging bodies did not look the part of biker guy or biker babe. So what! We still felt we had the stamina to give the trip a try.

Our biking experience consisted of a couple of rides in Thailand, but, at home, we only went out on sunny days to an upscale neighborhood where we would move at a slow pace to avoid hitting deer crossing the road or dodge the gardeners manicuring the lawns. We probably should have done some serious training, but working a full time job, I only had enough time to visit the gym each morning. Jim, being retired, had more time, but after his workout at the Y, he often needed a nap to get through the day. Our lack of physical energy throughout the day did not worry us since we planned to go slow and take as long as needed to reach our goal.

To get started, I did some research and found a company that sold cross-country cycling maps. I sent for the Lewis and Clark Trail because it went across the northern states from Oregon to North Dakota and then dipped south. We would be able to travel the safest roads until we reached Bismarck, and then we would have to find our own way across to Michigan. We had read that there were cycling routes along the Saint Lawrence River so we knew that once we got into Canada we wouldn't get lost.

Our first task was to locate our bikes, stored for the winter somewhere in the garage. Once they were unearthed and inspected for the requisite seat, handle bars, gears and wheels, we figured we simply had to pump up the tires, and we would be off. But then our youngest son, a serious biker, insisted we take the bikes into a shop to be serviced before heading out. Once there, while we waited for our bikes, we discovered all sorts of wonderful gear that the friendly salesman assured us were essential to the success of our trip. For example, how could we even think about cycling anywhere without the proper clothing?

Clothing? What was wrong with just rolling up a pant leg on our jeans, we asked the salesman. Shaking his head and chuckling to himself, he quickly steered us to the racks of bike shorts. "Of course you need shorts. They are padded. How long do you think you can sit on a bike seat without padding?" he asked.

So, I took a tiny pair of black spandex clearly built for a small child and headed into the changing room. After an epic struggle, I managed to get the shorts up to my waist. Sucking in my gut and looking in the mirror, I admired my now svelte figure, but as soon as I let out my breath the pants quickly rolled downward allowing my gut to pooch out and my pear shaped figure to re-emerge.

Jim tried on his shorts and thought they were a tad tight. I didn't have the heart to tell him that he was wearing what women of a certain age used to call girdles. It was obvious what had happened. When the evolution of women's clothing styles freed women from wearing foundation garments, the underwear industry had to find a way to unload all those unsold girdles. So, they dyed them black, added a little padding and sold them to sports outlets as bike shorts.

We bought the shorts, although I was skeptical about how a thin piece of padding tucked in the bottom would enhance seat comfort. Later when we were cycling every day across country the padding may well have helped. I never knew since my nether regions lost all feeling within an hour of chugging along. Instead, I heard those newly acquainted muscles in my back, my neck, my shoulders, my legs, my feet – my entire body – yelling in their shrill voices: Stop!

Before we could scurry out of the store, the ever so helpful salesman steered us to the cycling shirts. The salesman assured us that those flashy logo loaded tight fitting jerseys were a necessity. Anyone, who was a serious biker, wore them. Was he implying that we were not serious about our forthcoming ride? Well, we would show him. I trotted back into the dressing room and tried on this jersey and that. Neon yellow, bright red, carrot orange and Pepto-Bismol pink….all so cheerful and guaranteed to perk up our ride with the added benefit that we would be visible for miles. Unfortunately, no matter how hard I pulled and pushed and crammed by upper body into those jerseys, the end result was a disaster. Bulges here, bulges there, my tummy poking out from underneath. It was not a pretty sight. I finally settled for an XXXX large men's tee shirt in organic orange. It was long enough to cover my new bike shorts and my free-swinging gut. My husband also chose the organic orange, so that throughout our trip we could always identify each other in the distance looking like two lollipops bouncing down the road.

Dare To Do It!

   Having such great success, the salesman showed us helmets, gloves and sunglasses. He assured us that an aerodynamic helmet would help us move faster and with the wrap around sunglasses look oh so professional. We could hardly resist his logic.

   Now we were kitted out with the right clothes so that people seeing us passing by would remark, "Wow, look at those cool bikers; they must be really hard core." But as we tried to escape from the store, the salesman called us back. There were many more items we needed. Oh, yes, there was the GPS system, the strobe for the front, the blinking light for the back, the bento box for the cell, a compact camera bag for the front of the bike, a tire pump, an inner tube, a small CO_2 canister to pump up a flatten tire and energy gels of odd tasting mixtures, water bottles, racks to hold the bottles, bike gloves, sweat bands, and finally, bike shoes.

   We could hardly bike across the country without the special bike shoes that required the purchase of special bike pedals. How silly of us to assume we could wear ordinary sneakers. Clipped on shoes make our cycling more efficient we were told; however, the salesman failed to mention that detaching the shoe from the bike could be a bit tricky and, if not done early on before stopping, would result in a very uncomfortable sideways crash.

   Escaping the store, we hurried home to try out all our new purchases. We attached the equipment to our bikes, put on our new clothing and decided to take a spin around the block to check out our biking skills. The first problem I encountered was lifting my leg high enough to swing it over the seat saddle. The second problem was the bike pants. They were threatening to slide down my thighs, having already rolled below my tummy, so when I swung my leg over the seat, the crotch caught on the front of the seat and I was frozen with one leg in the air, one arm holding the handlebars and the other trying to pull up the pants enough to settle in the seat. I suddenly experienced horrendous cramps in my air borne leg, causing tears to well up in my eyes. When I finally managed to bring my leg back down and regained the use of said leg, I still had not mounted my bike. Finally, I followed Jim's lead and found a curb to stand on so that I didn't have to lift my leg so far to get it over the bike frame.

   Once on the bike, I tried to clip my shoes into the tiny bars that took the place of the pedals. After several tries I heard a clink and knew that at least one of my shoes was now welded to the bike. I pushed off and finally clipped the other shoe in as well. Pedaling down the driveway was okay, but when I came to the street and had to stop, I could not detach my foot quickly enough, and as I braked and lost momentum I simply fell over into the gravelly debris on the side of the street. Thank goodness there were no cars or people to see the sleek bike-clad me lying tangled in my bike unable to extract myself. I managed to reach over and pull my shoe straps open and remove my foot. But I was unable to pull my leg up over the bike seat and frame because of those agonizing muscle spasms. This would not be the first time or the last that my body would scream at me in protest. Some time later, my husband returned and lifted the bike and my bike shoes off of me and I was able to get up. Standing in my socks on the side of the road I inspected my left side. Not only was my upper thigh covered in huge purple bruises, but also it now sported an abstract design of tiny pebbles embedded in my skin. I decided to head for the back yard to practice clipping in and out of my bike on the lawn using the porch as a mini-launching pad.

Since we were unable to begin our trip until the middle of July, we were a little concerned that if our trip took too long we would undoubtedly hit bad weather. We planned to cycle only fifty miles per day so that we would not get too tired. We had never biked consecutive days ever and had no idea if we could do so. We knew we couldn't bike every other day as it would extend our trip into winter, and there was no way that we could possibly cycle in cold weather. Jim had asthma and would not be able to breath and cycle if the temperature dropped below fifty degrees. Doing some research we discovered that our bikes were too lightweight to carry any weight beyond that of our bodies. That meant that we either had to purchase new touring bikes or take our car and carry all our belongings in it. It was no big decision. We decided to drive our car and trade off cycling, while one of us acted as a support vehicle driver.

Having our car would give us a sense of safety against any negative events that we might encounter. Jim had heart surgery a few years back and might need to go to a hospital should he have any problems. The weather in the Mid West was well known for its tornadoes, hell storms and forest fires. We also decided that we would have to sleep in a hotel bed each night as our creaky old bodies would not be able to handle lying on a pad on the ground, and crawling out of a tent each morning. Driving our car and taking turns cycling was not a problem since we did not cycle at the same speed or distance. Riding those narrow shoulders and coping with traffic on the highways was enough of a problem to deal with. There would be no time to gab. Since we did not bike together I was only able to describe the trip from my perspective. Jim may have had some interesting experiences while he was cycling, but he never shared them with me. He never like riding with traffic and chose bike trails whenever possible while I was more of the risk taker and rode the highways.

Dare To Do It!

Our cycling adventure started at the beach in Seaside, Oregon. The busy streets were packed with tourists. The agile ones ran on the beach hanging onto kites that turned and twisted in the gusty wind. Along the streets the more sedentary people wandered in and out of shops looking for the perfect vacation souvenir.

At the famous Lewis and Clark statue, I planned to climb on my bike to begin our great North American adventure. Jim, driving the support vehicle, had parked outside of town to avoid the crowds. I stood for a moment watching clumps of people standing in the street oblivious to traffic, as they pushed and pulled family members into position for the perfect photo next to Lewis and Clark. It was clear that I would not be able to cycle through the groups, around the dogs or swerve to miss tiny children wandering every which way. I knew that Jim and I would probably not cycle every foot or mile of our journey, but I didn't expect it to happen before we had even started. I walked a couple of blocks away from the shoreline where I could finally mount my bike and begin cycling.

At the north end of town I turned inland, rode through a lush green valley and soon encountered a hill so vertical it looked as if one needed mountain climbing gear to reach the top. There was no chance on earth that I was going to make it up on my bike. One misstep would surely send me tumbling to the bottom. Not thirty minutes into our adventure, and I was not only crawling on all fours, but also hauling my bike along via my replacement inner tube, which I had slung over my shoulders and over the bike handles. Good thing I came prepared.

A half hour later I reached the top to find a level plateau, a country lane with no traffic and lovely rural scenery just as I had envisioned for this trip. But, of course, the quiet farmland quickly transformed into housing developments, busy streets and a scattering of small mom and pop stores.

I finally arrived in Astoria, famous as the location of Fort Clatsop where Lewis and Clark spent the winter of 1805-1806. We had planned to visit the fort, but after the "grand" start of our adventure, I was too tired to do anything but lie down and take a nap.

The next day, Jim took off for an hour of cycling while I waited in the car. The idea of taking turns with one person riding and one person ready to assist if necessary worked well later on in our trip, but on the highway from Astoria to Portland, the traffic was so heavy and distracting that Jim was happy to finish his hour and get off his bike and let me take my turn. As soon as I started I could see that this was not at all like riding in the quiet neighborhood streets at home.

All of a sudden, the shoulder seemed much too narrow, the cars too close and the huge trucks and motorhomes down right scary. However, I knew that lots of bikers did this route every year, so I told myself if they could do it, so could I.

When I came to a steep downhill grade, I smiled to myself thinking that if Jim had stayed on his bike a little bit longer, he could have chalked up the miles without any effort as he coasted to the bottom. Instead, I would put in at least three miles just hanging onto the handlebars and riding along effortlessly.

As I began the descent I immediately discovered that the shoulder disappeared with each curve of the road. When the first logging truck scraped by me leaving strings of bark swirling about my head, when the burst of wind from the vehicle grabbed my bike making it feel as if it were air borne, and when the noise of the truck horn pounded against my ear drums, I knew I was in deep trouble. My first reaction was to brake and slow down, but that only made my bike wobble uncontrollably. Then, after the logging truck came a motorhome, a double wide expandable monster that was so close, my bike was as frightened as I and clung to the road barrier. I did not dare move a single muscle, wiggle a toe, or even blink. I froze. The faster I went the tighter I held onto the handlebars until my hands and lower arms went numb. My feet lost all feeling as well. Into my head popped all sorts of scenarios of me flipping onto my side and sliding under the wheels of some huge SUV or sailing over the road barrier to fall hundreds of feet to the railroad tracks below where a train would come along before I could unclip my feet from the bike.

Fortunately, I made it to the bottom of the hill, and as the road curved off to the left, I coasted onto the verge and fell over into the gravel and grass. I might end up bruised and even a bit bloody, but I was alive. My hands were still so numb I had to peel them off the handlebars. But now, lying on my side, I had no leverage to push my shoes out of the clips holding them onto the bike. I looked up to see what I could do to right myself and as a bored but curious cow watched, I grabbed hold of the fence and both my bike and I jumped a couple of feet in the air. The jolt from the electric fence certainly helped to get the circulation going again. I should have known better when I saw the cow and the fence, but my thoughts were focused on the relief I felt having gotten off the road to safety. As I reached down to loosen my shoe, horrendous cramps and searing pain shot through my leg. Damn, I should have done some serious stretching before getting on the bike or would that have made any difference with my old worn-down body?

Every time I climbed on my bike, every time I fell over and every time I felt the cramps, the aches and the pain, I had to think about whether we old folks,

Jim and I, really could complete this trip. We had only been on the trip for two days and still had over four thousand miles to go and already my body was complaining. How in the world would we manage the next four months?

Finally, I was able to slide my feet out of the shoes and clamber upright. Standing in my socks I took several deep breaths, and looked over at the cow. I swear it was smirking! I yanked the bike shoes off the pedal bars, crammed my feet into the shoes and with grass sticking to my organic orange shirt, pedaled down the road until I came to a small community where there was a coffee hut. There sat Jim reading the paper and drinking a latte. "Where have you been all this time?" he asked. At that moment I decided that we needed some support vehicle rules, like actually paying attention to the person biking rather than snoozing or doing sudoku.

Crossing the river on the north side of Portland put us into Washington State where we planned to follow the Columbia River until it turned north. We would then continue east to Walla Walla before crossing into Idaho. With the huge number of logging trucks, semis and motor homes grazing our handle bars, sending up gusts of wind to destabilize our bikes and cutting us off at the curves, we huddled as close to the road edge as possible while our hearts pounded at ungodly rates. Jim was happy to do his hour and then let me take over the cycling because he was sure his recently installed pace maker would short circuit if he continued dodging vehicles on the road.

I wasn't excited about sharing the road with all those truckers, but figured it was time to harden myself to the realities of road riding. This traffic was bad, and undoubtedly we would encounter more as we journeyed across the country, but we either had to learn to cope with it or else give up our trip.

The stretch of road along the Columbia continued to climb upward, with long steep hills. Just about the time I thought I could go no further in the ninety-seven degree heat, the road crested and around the next curve was a drive-out where numerous cars had parked to take in the panoramic view of the mighty Columbia that shimmered in the sunlight thousands of feet below. In the hazy distance to the west was Mt. Hood poking its head into the clear blue sky. The sight was impressive and even more so when I realized just how far I had cycled from sea level to the top of this mountain, and I didn't have to walk, although I might have gotten to the top faster if I had. From the lookout the road began to descend until the route morphed into small rolling hills that serious bikers would call "flat," but for us oldsters still presented a challenge. At least the ups were short and the downs were shallow enough for some helpful coasting without the wobbles and worries of falling into traffic.

What a relief it was to return to sea level where the biking would be relatively easy. We had only been on the road a few days, and I was already welcoming the small hills that before our trip would have been considered challengingly steep. But the euphoria of being on "flat" ground did not make the cycling any easier. Ahead of us were several tunnels of varying lengths. Inside the tunnels, there were no shoulders and the narrow two lanes looked much too skinny to accommodate both a car and a bike much less two cars going in opposite directions.

In order to go through a tunnel I had to push a large button that would activate a blinking yellow light. Was this going to stop cars from running over me? Hardly. The vehicles zipped through the tunnels at high rates of speed. Jim wanted me to get in the car, but being stubborn, I decided I had to bike through. I waited until I could see no traffic from behind and then started pedaling fast, faster and fastest. Immediately the hot breath of a huge Mac truck whooshed across my back. I tried to increase my speed, my legs churning around in the "windmill," a racing technique our daughter, a triathlon competitor, had once suggested I use to increase my speed. I had never felt a need to use it until this moment when I could sense the huge truck bumper hugging my rear tire. Perhaps I wasn't doing the technique correctly because my legs seemed to be locked in first gear. I finally shot out of the first tunnel with a pounding heart, gasping breath and hands locked to the handlebars, but even though I could see daylight I was not able to relax as the road narrowed even further and the monster truck continued to bore down upon me. Finally, with a swish and a pat on my rear, the bumper swung out taking its truck past me. Before I could relax, a second truck came barreling up behind me honking its horn. I nearly jumped out of my skin but managed to stay on my bike. Several tunnels later, completely exhausted with nerves tingling and heart ready to burst from my chest, I was able to find the support vehicle on a small but deep shoulder. My legs were so shaky that Jim had to hold the bike while I dismounted and crawled into the car.

More challenges lay ahead. Having survived the tunnels and with traffic thinning, I thought that the cycling would get easier. Ha! The new challenge was the wind. Eastern Washington was relatively treeless, and it often felt like I was suspended in one spot pushing and pulling the pedals up and down to no avail. It seemed to take forever to make any progress. No matter how much I concentrated on the pavement, I couldn't resist counting telephone poles or road signs to see whether I had actually moved forward. Sometimes I would come across a sand dune that blocked the wind. Immediately my bike would straighten from its horizontal angle and the shock of being windless caused my bike to wobble in an inebriated series of curves out into the middle of the tarmac and back. Luckily no vehicles came along while I prodded my bike back to the side of the road. By then there was no more sand hill to block nature's force and a powerful gust of wind, again, blew me sidewise. For the next ten miles my bike creaked and groaned protesting the back and forth motion of wind and no wind. This was certainly not the way I envisioned crossing America.

As we journeyed along the southern edge of Washington State, we crossed over to Oregon for the night because that side of the Columbia was more developed and had many hotels from which to choose. At Hood River we watched the sail boarders using canopies to lift up into the air in graceful arcs. I would have loved to try the sport, but after sparing with the wind for most of the day, I was too tired. Jim preferred to watch the boarders from the side of the river.

We drove into Walla Walla on a Saturday to find the Walla Walla Sweet Onion Festival in progress. Booths lined the main street of town offering all kinds of tasty foods that were made with onions or had onion accompaniments. Before we could indulge our appetites, I wanted to have my hair trimmed to keep it from sticking to my face in the heat. We were lucky to find a place open on the weekend, and I willingly waited while the beautician finished a man's haircut. As soon as I sat in the barber's chair I should have realized that I was in the wrong place. The beautician spoke very little English, and I spoke no Spanish. However, with gestures I was confident that she understood what I needed. A half an hour later as I looked in the mirror I could see that my hair was a bit shorter than I had expected. After leaving the establishment, I jumped in the car and my husband's startled expression clearly signaled a problem, but he didn't say anything. After checking into our hotel and having the opportunity to scrutinize my new hair-do I understood his reaction. I had a man's crew cut with bangs. I felt like crying, not so much because of the bristles now sticking out of my head, which would undoubtedly keep my head cool under my bike helmet, but because before leaving home I had headed off to the beauty shop for a bleach and dye job to transform my dull gray hair to sunshine yellow. My pricey investment in "beautification" was now lying on the barber's floor. And what would I do when we wanted to eat in a restaurant, wear my helmet in the dining room, cover my head with a hanky, or just hold my head high and ignore the snickers and stares?

The next day we cycled out of Walla Walls and into Idaho. The transformation from dry barren hills to lush green forests was dramatic. Soon we were biking along a lovely river on a quiet secondary road that wound its way up and over the Rockies. Finally, we were biking as I had visualized with sun on our backs, blue skies, beautiful scenery and a quiet road. How could it get any better? It didn't.

Not long after starting up the highway that curled its way around evergreens, hugging the mountainside and providing dramatic drop-offs where tiny slivers of water shimmered far below, the peacefulness of the morning was shattered by multiple revving engines. At first they were far away, but soon the noise got louder and louder. Leather jacketed fellows with bushy beards came screaming up the road and quickly disappeared out of sight.

But as I came around the next bend I felt a shiver run through me. Ahead were two big brutish men, tattooed arms, long scraggly ponytails, leaning on their parked Harleys as the sun glinted off their wrap-around glasses. What could I do? If I took off my helmet maybe I would scare them away. I was pedaling just fast enough to create a breeze to keep me reasonably cool, but that pace was so slow that a walker could easily overtake me. And now I was heading right for trouble.

Fortunately, I had a bigger imagination than was warranted. As I approached, the two men began to giggle and joke about my incredible speed. When I got closer and they could see I was an old lady, they found this even funnier. They made silly remarks: "Way to go granny?" "Keep up the speed and maybe you will make it to the top tomorrow!" They were laughing so hard that I easily passed them while they stood in the road bent over in paroxysms of laugher.

On I road at my snail's pace but continuing upward and hoping that around the next bend would be the top. Soon the two Harley riders passed by me their "whoopees" echoing through the mountain valleys. But then around the next bend, there sat the two Harley guys waiting for me to pass again. They stuck out their thumbs like hitchhikers and thought they were hilariously funny. I asked them if they wanted to trade bikes, but they found my remarks even funnier, laughing so hard that their Santa bellies jiggled up and down while tears rolled down their cheeks.

A few minutes later, they revved up their engines, passed by with a wave and a shout and disappeared forever. The quiet peacefulness of the morning had returned, and I could continue my slow progress uphill. By this time I was tired and had to resort to my mantra, one I used whenever I felt challenged. It was simple: "I think I can, I think I can, I know I can, I know I can." These simple phrases from a children's picture book about an engine that had to go over a mountain has stayed with me all of my life and helped me complete tasks that seemed at first to be impossible. And as I chanted to myself and continued on, the minutes and hours ticked by and finally I came around a bend, the road leveled out and I was at the top of the first pass over the Rockies.

Dare To Do It!

Later that afternoon we stopped in a small community where there was a coffee shop with Internet. I looked on line for lodging, since our bike route through the mountains was remote, and we were worried that we would have difficulty finding a place that was close by. Luckily, we found a narrow road that seemed to go up into the clouds, and at the top of this mini-mountain we found a horse ranch. With panoramic views it appeared to be an ideal setting. While most of the guest came to stay several days to take pack trips into the backcountry, the proprietors had one room still available that we could use for the night.

That next morning after a delicious breakfast, we were invited into the living room that was separated by a set of stairs. Once there, we had planned to talk with the other guests, but as we entered the room we were distracted by the décor. The entire room was filled to overflowing with stuffed animals: full size animals on the floor and smaller animals attached to platforms high on the walls poised as if they were about to attack. Any space not already occupied had animal heads. There were also birds with wings outspread as if to take flight. Both Jim and I found this menagerie disturbing, but we were even more distressed when we saw a full size giraffe attached to a doorway. In addition to the animals, there were pictures of the proprietor and his wife proudly posing over their kill. The owner was proud of his big game hunting and enjoyed describing his trips to the other guests. He justified his hunting because he said the animals had to be culled or they would die anyway. If we had known about the animals we would have never stayed at the lodge. Apparently the other guests did not share our discomfort as most of them were asking questions and making comments that suggested that they approved of what he said.

That morning we biked our usual fifty miles, and as we approached Missoula began seeing signs advertising a Testicle Festival. At first I assumed I had misread the signage, but after seeing more signs, I googled the Internet that evening and discovered that there really was such a festival featuring two contests: a wet tee shirt contest for women and drop the drawers for the biggest testicles for men. Somehow neither of these sounded appealing to us, and I think the partygoers might not find either my husband or I good candidates for either contest. So we ignored the turnoff and kept going through glorious mountain scenery.

Western Montana is strikingly beautiful set against the Rockies, but as we continued on into the eastern part of the state all we could see was dry brown land of rolling hills with clumps of small trees here and there. The landscape seemed to be devoid of habitation: no houses, no animals and only a few dirt roads that had no beginning and disappeared around hillsides going who knows where.

We stayed a couple of days in Missoula, and, while there learned that the northern bike route we had planned to follow had been compromised by the

Bakken Bonanza, a major fracking development. The two-lane highway had become a traffic nightmare, especially when huge construction trucks came hurdling down upon us. The locals were excited about the new oil discovery, and the local papers were full of upbeat stories about how everyone was going to get rich. Clearly this was no place for cycling, so we decided to head south.

Tracing our fingers along the north-south highways of our Montana map, we found a tiny thread of a road that squiggled here and there suggesting little traffic since there were other routes going south that looked much straighter. After leaving town, we headed east until we found the road we had marked on our map. Jim didn't like the narrow shoulders, so he suggested I started out first. The route looked promising: a lovely valley lined with old farmhouses and barns, some looking like they had been there for centuries. We had finally found the perfect country lane where we could cycle at leisure bonding with nature. After all the tension and stress of the previous weeks through the mountains, we had finally found our ideal bike route. Of course, it didn't last.

Not ten minutes into the ride a gargantuan Mac truck came barreling around a corner headed straight for me. The two-lane road was so narrow that the massive vehicle took up not only the roadway but the shoulders as well. The seconds seemed like an eternity as I pedaled ever faster to get to the one dirt road off to the right where I would be safe. I forced my creaky old legs to work harder than they had ever worked before, and in a swirl of dust and debris the truck passed within inches of my rear tire. I was so dazed that I forgot about the damn pedal clips and the next thing I knew I was staring up at the sky, my left side imprinted with pebbles, rocks and dirt and my legs screaming "cramp." I slowly wiggled my feet out of the shoes and clamored to an upright position and then finally to standing, but my legs were shaking so much I had to sit down again. As I sat there trying to get composed, several other huge road construction trucks flew past. I called Jim on my cell to pick me up. We drove the not-so-quiet road all the way to the Interstate.

The freeway was a welcome change since it had car-width shoulders and two lanes in either direction. Eastern Montana along the Interstate was filled with a sameness of landscape that made this part of our trip one of the most challenging. At least biking the freeway was the quickest way across the never-ending ranchland, but it was so monotonous that I never felt a sense of progress. Everything looked the same mile after mile.

Semi trucks tooted their horns acknowledging us as they moved to the inner lanes, and we waved back appreciating their thoughtfulness. But the motor homes were a different story. Most of them not only rode the outer lane but often used part of the shoulder as well. With the sameness of the landscape it was easy to fall into a "biker's high" and as I waltzed along, the rhythmic pedaling became hypnotic and the energy flowed, and I felt as if I were Icarus flying in the sky oblivious to any danger…that is until a motorhome passed. Suddenly, with its side mirror scraping every so close to my head, my waltz became a jitterbug as gusts of wind picked me up, twirled me around and broke the spell jolting me back to reality. I slowly regained my rhythm until another motorhome came whizzing by.

Sometimes the traffic thinned, and I enjoyed the steady rhythmic pedaling that put me in a comfortable stupor, not fully awake but enough to stay upright and move forward. At times there would be an interlude when there was no traffic at all. This lasted for several minutes. It was a strange feeling to be out there in the middle of a never-ending landscape with no one around. It made me think about another time when we were biking all alone without any traffic, only then we were in a city in northern Thailand. Asian cities are normally packed with vehicles coming and going, but on this particular day it was different.

We were living in Chiang Rai up near the Mekong River where we found the weather more agreeable than in Bangkok. When we visited a local bike shop the owner, who spoke a little English, told us about a bike event happening that next Sunday.

We thought he said that the tour was set up for foreigners, but that was not the case. When we arrived early on the designated day, there were hundreds of participants, all Thai, who appeared to belong to different bike clubs, as they clustered together according to the color of their tee shirts. The majority of the riders were young men, and they all had fancy racing bikes and numerous pieces of electronic gear attached to their handlebars. We were definitely out of our element and probably would not be able to keep up with these macho men. We noticed many puzzled looks since we were clearly oldsters and foreigners as well. Somehow the owner of the bike shop had failed to tell us that this was a religious event. We lined up at the back of the pack planning to start out with them but expecting to be quickly left behind.

After some time had passed, a group of dancers and musicians appeared. The dancers were dressed in traditional costumes, and when the music began, they gracefully swayed this way and that apparently telling some kind of story. After they finished their performance, a man gave a speech that was rather long and boring as evidenced by the bikers around us who were talking and laughing.

Suddenly, the bikers cheered and took off zipping out into the street ignoring the performers who scurried to get out of the way. We followed as best we could. By the time we had ridden across the field where the dancers had performed and ridden into the street, we could only see multicolored flashes of clothing several blocks away. It looked like we had been left behind at the start line. We decided to cycle in the direction of the bikers but with little hope of catching up to them. As we pedaled along we were surprised that there was no traffic. When we came to our first intersection we saw police barricades and patrolmen holding back the traffic in all directions. It was a puzzlement.

After traversing several blocks, to our amazement, there were all the bikers. They had turned into a temple compound. By the time we arrived all we could see were a mass of bikes and shoes piled on the ground. The cyclists were just coming out of a temple, putting on their shoes and lining up for a photo. Someone unfurled a huge banner, draped it in front of the group and said something to make everyone smile as he took a photo. Then the bikers climbed on their bikes and swarmed out into the street and rushed off for several blocks before turning into another temple compound and repeating the same process. After several more temples with Jim and I managing to catch up just as the group had finished their religious visits, we came to a steep hill. The fancy dressed cyclists on their high tech bikes no longer looked so hard-core. Most of them had to dismount and push their bikes up the steep incline. By the time I had walked my bike up the hill, the bikers had finished their temple visit and started down another hill back into town. At that point I realized that Jim was nowhere to be seen.

After waiting until the last of the bikers had put on his shoes and started down the hill, I decided that Jim probably never attempted the steep incline and was probably at the bottom. I followed the bikers as they flew down the hill and into a maze of streets, turning this way and that. By then I lost sight of the group, and I had no idea where Jim was. And I didn't know where I was either. Since the street was blocked off from traffic, I figured that if I continued on I would eventually find someone who would point me in the right direction.

After several blocks, I turned a corner and there was a remarkable sight. Jim was pedaling at his usual snail's pace in the middle of a major intersection. There was a motorcycle cop on one side of him and a policeman on a bicycle on the other side, otherwise, he was alone. People had climbed out of their cars and were standing behind the barricades watching Jim's progress. It was a great relief to see that he was okay. I followed behind the threesome until we came to a large stupa set in a traffic island. The tour group was just unfurling their banner and when they saw Jim, they all cheered and beckoned for the two of us to join them for the last photo of the tour. Our five minutes of fame! When we later described our experience to our son, who lives in Bangkok, he told us that the day was a major religious holiday, and the bike rally was undoubtedly celebrating it. What a surprise it was to tour the entire city without traffic.

The traffic free streets of Chiang Rai were entirely due to the efforts of the police, but in Montana, the police were not so accommodating. Every time a state patrol car passed us we expected to be pulled over. It was our understanding that cycling on a freeway was illegal and only acceptable if there is no other viable route. There was a two-lane highway that crossed Montana far to the north where most bikers would have headed, so we had no excuse to be on the Interstate.

Every time Jim took his turn to cycle he managed to find a level section of the highway. I found that rather strange until I discovered his secret. While sitting in the support vehicle it was clear he was not just doing his sudoku, he was studying the bike maps marking the routes with the least amount of elevation. After each ride he would rave on about the joys of leisurely riding. He always rode in the mornings before the temperature rose into the nineties. By the time I started riding I had to face a hot wind, lots of hills and all those people who slept in and now were out on the road.

As we moved further east I noticed the hills got steeper. Clearly Montana slanted uphill all the way to the border, or perhaps it was just that the biking was getting harder when the hot wind was constantly blowing into our faces. When we stopped for the day at a hotel, Jim would take a nap and I would work on the computer. By getting up at four a.m. and working during the mornings and then working in the afternoons while Jim napped, I was able to put in my forty-hour workweek. Sometimes, if I got behind, we would stay an extra day in a town. Then, in the mornings we would cycle together to the city park where there was usually a bike/running track. It was a great change from worrying about the traffic on the Interstate.

The expansive landscape of eastern Montana made most people think the state was flat so the biking would be easy. But, in fact, the highway undulated up and down with some dips so deep that after plunging down to the bottom I would not have the momentum to cycle out and ended up pedaling furiously to no avail as my bike refused to hitch itself up over the crest of the hill. Being clipped in with those damn bike shoes I would fall sidewise. At least with the wide shoulder I had the option of falling either right or left. I alternated.

As I trudged along, feeling the massiveness of that famous Montana sky above, I felt so tiny and insignificant like a resident of Whosville. Was there an entity, like Horace looking down and watching us tiny earthlings going about our lives? If so, he might wonder why we had taken on such a thankless task as traversing America on a bike, for god sakes, when a car, a bus or plane could do the crossing so much more quickly and efficiently. It didn't help to have the hot breath of the wind constantly blowing in our faces making it feel as if we were pushing against a wall.

Although we stayed at hotels along the Interstate we did explore some of the towns that were often situated a few miles away from the highway. Most towns in this part of the state appeared to be wind blown clusters of low-lying buildings. There was such a sameness to the town features that once, years ago, when we were driving across Montana and bored with the usual meals in the fast food joints, we took a secondary road north from the freeway stopping for breakfast in a small town with one main street. All the buildings were closed except for a diner where the cluster of vehicles around the building suggested good eats inside. At the front door we could hear lots of loud talking and camaraderie. But as soon as we entered, the noise stopped and in the complete silence we could see all these men staring at us. We felt like aliens from another planet. A server did direct us to a table and slowly the men returned to their conversations, but they continued to send hostile looks in our direction.

I glanced around and noticed that there were only men in the establishment. They wore rumpled, plaid shirts, mud-encrusted blue jeans, sweated-stained cowboy hats and scruffy cowboy boots. These were authentic cowboys, not those softies wearing fancy white shirts for good and black for evil. These cowboys didn't look like they would be interested in saving a damsel in distress. Instead, they looked like they had just come in from herding a couple hundred cows across the Western plains. Despite the cool welcome, calloused hands served us the best greasy spoon fair we have ever eaten.

When we lived in Australia we had a similar experience only with a less desirable ending. Jim and I went into a bar to get a beer, but the minute we stepped across the threshold all the men inside stopped talking and stared at us. Their conceited swagger, their sunburnt faces mottled with red dirt from the outback, and their barnyard odor strong enough to knock my socks off, all made it clear that this was a man's world. And, indeed, it was. The bartender blocked our entrance and told us if we wanted a drink to go around to the back. Sure enough, in the back of the tavern we found a small door and an even smaller sign saying, "Ladies with Escorts Only." We went in and drank a beer, but it wasn't really that much fun sitting all alone in a room without windows while we could hear the men laughing and joking at the front of the building.

The distrust of strangers in Montana and that of women in Australia seemed to me related to the rugged isolated landscape of both places. On this biking trip Jim and I would have liked to stop again in that little town just to see if things had changed and perhaps the people would be more welcoming, but with the possibility of a change in the weather forever on our minds, we clung to the Interstate staying in hotels and restaurants that were carbon copies of each other and where no one questioned the gender of its guests. There certainly were no authentic cowboys here.

We finally came to Glendive, the most eastern town in Montana. I was surprised to learn that the town produced caviar. Who would have known that out here in this dusty little down we would find such gourmet fare? We decided to purchase a case of the delectable treats to take home as gifts to our friends. We discovered that the caviar was not readily available in the local stores and that the Chamber of Commerce handled the product. That seemed strange to us, but we decided to go there and see what they had to say. Surprisingly, the office clerk told us that the town did sell caviar but rarely to customers in the U.S. She said that over three thousand fishermen came to snag Paddlefish, a prehistoric creature that lives in the Yellowstone River. The Chamber paid the fishermen to collect the fish eggs, which were processed into caviar and then sent to Japan. Even though the caviar was produced domestically it still cost over eighty dollars for a two-ounce jar. The clerk said that there was one jar left if I wanted it. At that price, I decided to find some other gifts to take home to family and friends.

Cycling across Montana was not without its problems. Bouncing along in my meditative state I didn't notice when the front light fell off. It was not until I stopped many miles down the road that I discovered the loss. I could not believe that I did not see it when it was directly in front of me. Uninterrupted pedaling that induced a meditative state was okay on long stretches but could have dangerous consequences. One time I was jolted to attention when a semi truck suddenly appeared in front of me at an exit ramp. No argument there. I just pedaled down the exit ramp too, until the truck had passed by. However, on the shoulders of the ramps, vehicles often left tiny corkscrews of metal thrown off as they passed by. These could worm their way into a bike tire and cause a flat. I was lucky to have only one such occurrence. We simply stopped at the nearest bike shop where the repairman fixed the tire in a couple of minutes. Jim and I had learned how to change a tire, but it would have taken us an hour or more.

As we moved east and got closer to North Dakota, the hotels were a hive of activity. It seemed as if every building was being renovated. We even got up one morning to loud activity in the hallway to find a man standing nearby propping up a door that he wanted to put on the very room we were occupying. Apparently the door on our room was made out of some kind of cardboard. If we had known the door was easily breached we might have worried for a while, but with all the exercise we were getting, we both would not have been able to stay awake long enough to scare away any would-be intruders. We were at least a hundred miles from the oil fields, but it was clear that the people here were hoping to become rich renovating and adding onto existing hotels for the anticipated increase in workers and tourists. The front page of the local papers reported daily news from the "Bakken Bonanza" oil fields and enterprising locals even offered tours to see the oilrigs in action.

As we headed into North Dakota, the landscape changed. The ranch land gave way to farms. Cows and corn were now the new scenery. Where the cornfields had been harvested, the wind blew sideways in gusts that made staying on the road difficult. The wind blew so hard at times that it seems as if my bike was side stepping first left and then right depending upon whether there were buildings to block the wind or open fields where the wind could have its way. Progress was slow, but I had not realized how slow until I encountered a cow that broke away from the gossipers around the water trough, wandered over to the fence and ambled along the fence line accompanying me. Clearly bored, the cow would stare at me with its soulful eyes wondering what I was doing working so hard in the noon heat. The cow kept pace with me until it reached the fence barrier. Real bikers keep track of their progress with some kind of fancy GPS device, but I could pace myself by the speed of a cow. Clearly I would not win any cross-country bike race. But, at least I was moving fast enough for a slight breeze to keep me from overheating in the ninety-degree temperature. Still, sweat would gather under my helmet and soak my headband and then begin to trickle down my face. By the time I stopped for the day my organic orange tee shirt was soaked as if I had dipped it in a bucket of water.

After passing miles of the yammering cows and rustling cornfields, we came upon a most unusual sight. The land had been relatively flat with just shallow dips here and there so it was a surprise to suddenly see a vast canyon made up of multi-colored bands of sandstone pinnacles whose shapes changed dramatically as the sun cast shadows on one side or the other. This was Teddy Roosevelt State Park, a marvelous natural wonder. Standing on the rim of this miniature Grand Canyon we could watch for hours, if we had the time, as the shifting sun changed the colors of each layer of earth. In the far distance we noticed an oilrig. Was it possible that the oil companies were drilling here, in a state park? Apparently, the rangers were worried that big business was going to compromise this beautiful landscape. There were articles in the local newspapers speculating about the effects of fracking. Would it cause earthquakes, and, if so, would it damage these spectacular sandstone structures?

Cycling at a slow pace enable us to study roadside attractions that might otherwise go unnoticed if one were passing by in a car. Just outside Bismarck we saw the largest cow statue in the world and not much further on the largest bison in the world. But that wasn't all! In the visitor's center in Fargo, there was on display a wood chipper with a leg sticking out of it, a leftover prop from the popular movie, *Fargo*. The folks in North Dakota have a great sense of humor albeit a bit macabre. Perhaps the cow and bison statues were an attempt at the state's fifteen minutes of artistic fame? Surely, the wood chipper plus leg would guarantee it.

After Bismarck, we continued going east on the Interstate. Up until now we had been encountering cyclists heading west on the Lewis and Clark Bike Trail. They would have started in Missouri, headed north to Bismarck and then turned west. The cyclists would wave and encourage us, and we waved back. Sometimes we even had a chance to stop and talk briefly. There were lots of groups biking with support vans, couples following each other loaded with packs on the front and back of their bikes, and single riders, always males. One fellow we talked to had a bamboo bike he had built. He said that when he stopped at a truck-weighing machine his bike and equipment added up to over two hundred-fifty pounds. That would have been too much for Jim and me to haul down the road. It made us ever so happy that we decided to take turns cycling and carry our belongings in the car.

In contrast to the countryside, the urban centers in North Dakota were lively, leafy and lovely. We found a wonderful bike trail on the outskirts of Fargo that bordered the river that divides North Dakota and Minnesota. The trail wove its way through glorious old trees whose green canopy shaded us from the glaring sun and created a peaceful haven of serenity, save for the occasional piercing scream of some baby in a stroller and an equally screaming mother trying to quiet the wee one. This was such a contrast to the overdeveloped paved congestion near the highway where the hotels and restaurants stood row upon row.

We finally entered Minnesota, a state that claims to have ten thousand lakes, but fails to mention the ten million mosquitoes that live along the shores. With the wind blowing off the lakes the bugs were not a problem. But when we were on a trail in the woods where the wind was blocked by the trees, any small pond was clearly a habitat for these irksome creatures. As soon as we showed up swarms of the buggers swirled around the head, diving into and out of ears, crawling across the sunglasses and sometimes even trying to climb into the nose. Now I understood why so many houses had screened porches.

The multitude of bike trails was amazing. There were trails constructed from old railroad beds that were long, straight and often enclosed by dense forests. And then there were roller coaster trails along side most highways that were marked with traffic signs that indicated that they were for snowmobilers. In any case, with both trails available for recreational purposes, people of all sizes and shapes were out walking, jogging, running or biking. It was a wonderful thing to see so many people enjoying the outdoors. I found the snowmobile trails amusing since many of the traffic signs said to reduce speed to ten miles per hour. If only I could get my pedaling up to ten miles an hour!

The former railroad bed trails were not marked with any signage. The only way we knew we had arrived at a town was when we saw the local tavern on one side of a street and the church directly across from it. Usually I could tell when I was close to a town by the increased traffic. Mothers with young children and at least one dog would be wandering here and there. Some women had strollers; others simply walked along chatting to each other ignoring their tots who were running back and forth across the trail in haphazard fashion. This always created a problem. Should I stay on my bike and try to out guess the directions the little kids were heading or unclip and walk pass the group. No matter what decision I made it was never the right one. Walking meant having a dog nipping at my bare legs. Riding meant weaving between bodies of ladies who often looked surprised to encounter me.

Out of town a mile or two the trees leaned in and the branches reached out to entangle their arms in a leafy embrace providing a canopy under which we could ride protected from the sun. At first this was welcome as the forest was quiet and remote without the noisiness found in the towns. But it didn't take long for the old brain cells to start working overtime when a shadow on my right seemed to move or a glance on my left suggested an animal of some kind. Soon my head was full of "what-ifs." What if the chain saw murderer was skulking in the woods? Fargo wasn't that far away, and who knows if there might be a copycat murderer out there with his/her own personal wood chipper? What if it were a hungry bear? Someone told us before we set out on the trails that bears were often sighted in the woods, and it was getting toward fall, so they would be wanting to fatten up for their winter hibernation. A tender biker might be just the tasty morsel it was looking for. What if a tire blew, and I had to walk for miles to the nearest outlet after having biked forty miles. There were a few times when I had to rein in my bike as we both jumped at least a foot in the air at the sound of rustling in the woods and my overactive imagination.

Once I came across a snake coiled in the middle of the trail in a patch of sunlight. By the time my mind had registered the possible danger, I was on top of it. My ankle grazed the head. Luckily, it didn't react until I had passed by. It was an unsettling experience because it brought back memories of another time when I had encountered a snake that had terrified me.

I had mentioned that Jim and I traveled with our son and his wife to visit their daughter in Penang, and while there we had gone to a popular park where the monkeys were very aggressive. What I didn't mention was my snake experience.

Behind the park was Penang Hill, a steep mini-mountain with a funicular train for tourists on one side and a steep road used by the locals on the other side. My son decided to hike up the road, and I decided to accompany him. I tried to keep up but soon fell behind, and he disappeared around a bend. It was late afternoon, and, as I gasped for breath, I realized that I would not make it to the top, and I needed to retrace my steps back down the hill. As I turned around I saw an enormous snake dangling from a tree in front of me. A jogger passing by told me to hurry as after dark hundreds of snakes dropped from the trees to the ground. I don't know if he was joking or not, but I ran faster than I have ever done. Stumbling and falling, I flew to the bottom of the mountain. I am sure my feet never touched the ground. I didn't know I could move so fast!

The next day Jim and I went to the same hill but to the other side where the funicular train took us up to an observation platform for a panoramic view of Georgetown and the ocean beyond. Near the platform two young men had set up a tent where they offered to take our picture holding a snake that they had captured. When the men draped the huge creature over our shoulders I shuddered not because of this snake that was probably drugged, but it reminded me of the snake dangling from the trees that I had encountered the day before. We sat down, held our breaths and smiled and the process turned out to be quick and painless. The skin on the snake actually felt rather pleasant, not at all what I imagined it would be like. The Minnesota snake may not have been as large as the Asian one, but it still made my heart beat triple time.

Besides snakes, the Minnesota forests were inhabited by a variety of wildlife. I saw a bear wandering along the trail up ahead. Naturally, I slowed down and, focusing on the potential danger, came to a stop and fell sideways smacking the ground. It was a great technique. The noise of my body hitting the pavement and my unexpected yelp sent the bear running. The occasional deer would leap over the trail in one liquid motion flashing its hooves in the air as it disappeared into the brush. Rabbits would jump out unexpectedly, take one look at the crazy biker and were gone in seconds. But there were two animals that were the biggest problem of all - turtles and squirrels.

For whatever reason turtles liked to migrate from one body of water to another. To do so, they crossed the bike trail. I encountered these dinner-plate sized animals sitting in the middle of the pathway half hidden by forest debris. The problem was that I never saw them until I was nearly on top of them. I managed to swerve through the hard-shelled obstacle course wobbling in large loops to avoid hurting them. Often I found myself on the edge of the trail where I risked falling into the very water from which the turtles had come - or were going.

But of all the animals that were lurking in the woods, the most "dangerous" animal was the squirrel. It would be interesting to know just what went on in its little mind. It ran out of the bush, stopped in the middle of the trail, ran this way, turned around and ran a short distance the other way and then turned around again. It was impossible to figure out which way the animal would finally go. Naturally, to avoid hitting it, I turned this way and that, trying to outguess it. As I careened back and forth before regaining control and getting back to a steady rhythm, some biker would appear and, finding it difficult to pass, would yell something unprintable about my lack of biking ability.

Many of the towns we encountered, were proud of their Scandinavian heritage and had huge folk hero statues in their parks. Bemidji, where we stayed for a couple of days had the famous Paul Bunyan and Babe, his blue ox, statues. These were real crowd pleasers as tourists lined up by the dozens to get their pictures taken standing underneath the huge creature or next to Paul Bunyan's big boot. The town's location on a large lake attracted the wind that blew constantly at gale force. We managed to get in twenty miles riding around the lake, but, on one side, the wind was so strong, we felt as if we were on stationary bikes going nowhere. We inched along while turtles passed us. Finally, we were able to make it back to the hotel. Exhausted, we flopped down on the bed still in our bike gear and slept until the next morning.

In one small town I took off on the only trail going out of town and, as I swerved around the turtles, dodged the squirrels and began to get the rhythm for a good long ride, my cell rang. My heart began to beat fast as I fumbled around trying to locate it. We only used our cells for emergencies, so, of course, I was worried that something awful had happened to Jim. But it was not Jim who was in trouble, it was I. Jim said I was lost. I didn't feel lost, as the trail had no inlets or outlets so it seemed impossible for me to heading the wrong way. My options were to retrace my ride, some twenty miles, or continue on until I came to a town. I chose to continue on, and eventually I spied the requisite tavern, church and "Big Olie" statue. Since there was no signage I had to ask a local for the name of the town. I called Jim and he came to my rescue.

One of the trails we cycled was entitled, "Lake Wobegon." The trail looked to be pretty much like all the other trails, and I didn't see any "women who were strong, men who were good looking, and children who were above average" as Garrison Keillor claimed in *Prairie Home Companion*. I was too busy dodging dogs, toddlers and an assortment of tricycles and baby buggies.

One night a storm came through the town. It was loud and scary as the thunder roared and lightning lit up the sky. It poured so heavily I was worried it might turn to hail and ruin the car. Living in the Northwest we do not have such spectacular storms so it was exciting to watch from the safety of the hotel room but frightening to hear.

We got up the next morning to heavy clouds, some black and inky and others shades of gray. After working all morning while Jim slept, we decided to go out cycling before the weather got worse. The clouds looked threatening, and the wind was gusty and very powerful. I thought we might get blown over at times. We rode down lanes near the hotel and managed to get in ten miles before the clouds opened up and threw buckets of rain at us. This was the first foul weather we encountered on the entire trip. It made us think about how quickly fall was approaching and whether we would experience more bad weather especially as we were heading north into Canada and out to the mouth of the St. Lawrence River on the Atlantic Ocean.

When it was my turn to be the support vehicle driver, I always found some place where I could park that was completely off the road, and that meant that sometimes I ended up parked at a junction with some secondary road. One time when I was sitting in the car waiting for Jim to appear, a state patrol car passed, turned around and came up beside me. He looked very skeptical when I told him what I was doing, and he hung around for a good twenty minutes. Finally, he drove off but passed by several more times. A good half hour later I saw in the distance a bright organic orange blob slowly moving along. I wished that patrolman had passed by one more time to see Jim so that he would know I wasn't lying.

One day we checked into a hotel on the Mississippi River, and, as I signed in, I mentioned that we were biking across the country to celebrate our fiftieth wedding anniversary. Hearing that, the reservation agent took away the original key she had handed me and gave me a different one telling me to "enjoy." How strange I thought, until Jim and I opened the door to our room. It was a conference room with two bedrooms, two big screen televisions, several couches, a conference table for six and a kitchenette stocked with drinks of all kinds. We could get lost in this place! The view from the wall of windows facing the river were dramatic, especially as the sun set and the shadows played across the trees lining the esplanade next to the river. Gazing about this massive room, larger than our entire house, I could not help but wonder just what kind conferencing happened here!

The upscale hotel room was a marvelous treat. Jim could watch sports on his big screen television in one room, and I could watch something else on my own big screen. If we were not so concerned about the weather, we would easily have stayed a few extra days.

We cycled south into Roseville, an outlying community of Minneapolis. It had quiet streets for biking and best of all, when we were finished with our cycling, we were always offered freshly baked cookies that the hotel staff had set out for all the guests. We spent several days exploring the neighborhoods and Northwestern University campus. We had planned to stay longer, but the receptionist told us that the hotel rate would double the next day because the state fair was to begin that weekend. Naturally, we had no choice but to leave. So we headed over to St. Paul.

On the eastern side of St. Paul we found a hotel that was near a golf course and a nature preserve. We reserved a room for an entire week because the quiet upscale neighborhood offered excellent biking. As soon as we had stowed our belongings in the room we headed out for an exploratory ride. Just as we were remarking on how perfect the cycling was, a vehicle came barreling around a corner and headed right for us. It veered onto the shoulder, but just before impact we were able to turn onto a side alley out of harm's way. Jim and I were shaken, but, after taking a few moments to relax, we turned around and started back down the street. A few moments later another car came up behind us, honked its horn and drove onto the shoulder forcing us into a shallow ditch that we managed to negotiate without falling over. When we tried to continue biking a third car came speeding toward us. We were dumbfounded. It was clear that people in this neighborhood did not like cyclists. This was a far cry from the friendly faces we had encountered in Minneapolis. The state advertised itself as the most bike friendly place in the union, but someone forgot to tell the people living in St. Paul. We continued to bike each day but cycled the sidewalks.

One day, Jim lay down for his usual afternoon nap while I was working. Having heard an unusual amount of noise outside the window, I went over and leaned out. Two police cars came into the parking lot, and out climbed four officers. They walked over to a small compact parked in one corner of the lot, all the time talking and laughing as if they were simply visiting. Shortly, an ambulance arrived. The men stood around talking for several more minutes and then, pulling on latex gloves, proceed to pry the doors of the compact open. After several minutes more of casual talk and even some laughter, the police and attendants pulled a man out and lifted him onto a gurney. After they covered the body with a sheet, they shoved it into the ambulance.

I had never seen a crime scene before, so I was disappointed that there was no perky young stiletto heeled Barbie doll giving orders; no handsome sidekick drooling over the gal; no yellow crime scene tape marking off the area, and no person taking pictures. Clearly, these guys needed to watch some television to learn the ropes. Finally after another twenty minutes of casual conversation sprinkled with laughter, the ambulance left while the police continued to stand around. I got bored and went back to work. Later that evening after Jim and I had returned from eating dinner at a nearby restaurant, we looked out to see the compact was gone. True crime isn't nearly as interesting as on television.

Another day after biking Jim and I entered the hotel lobby to chaos. There were dogs running every which way: big dogs and little dogs yapping, jumping on the furniture and having a great time while several ladies were chasing them here and there. Finally, the dogs were rounded up and put back in their cages while the women were going on and on about the dogs' hair-dos. Apparently, the dogs were headed to a dog show and had been groomed and fluffed for their moment of stardom, and now the ladies worried they would not have time to re-groom the dogs before show time.

After leaving the Twin Cities, we headed to Stillwater, a very lovely but highly popular tourist town on the Mississippi. Because the village tumbles down a steep hill into a main street and river front promenade, we decided to find a hotel on the highway where we could cycle along the hilltop. Going into the town on our bikes would mean a really miserable climb, or walk, back up the steep hillside. We did drive into the center of town and found some fantastic riverside restaurants where we could indulge in carbs and sweets, justifying the food because we were now cycling fifty to sixty miles each day. When we stayed in one location like this, Jim and I biked together taking our time enjoying the lovely scenery. I was proud of Jim, who had increased his daily cycling distance from ten to twenty miles. The downside to his longer rides was that he complained about his butt hurting. I found that interesting because I had other aches and pains that were much worse, like hot feet. When the temperature was in the eighties and nineties my feet began to burn as if walking on hot coals. I did all kinds of mental exercises to put the pain out of my mind, but sometimes I simply have to stop biking, dismount and take off my shoes. The pain was well beyond any that I felt from sitting on a bike seat.

One afternoon returning from a long cycle on a lovely forested bike path, I encountered Jim pedaling along at such a slow pace I thought sure he would topple over. It turned out that he had a slow tire leak. By the time he reached the hotel, he had a flat tire. We felt fortunate that we had no other mechanical problems considering that we had covered at least two thousand miles. We stopped at a bike shop and had a new inner tube installed. It took all of ten minutes, but if we had tried to do the repair it would have taken us over an hour.

After leaving Stillwater, Minnesota, we headed east into Wisconsin, stopping to visit Jim's relatives. Each year on Labor Day the Rubesch clan gathered for an annual picnic. The food was good, the talk was lively, and, happily, all of Jim's siblings were still in good health.

Jim and I were happy to see our daughter had come from San Francisco to attend the picnic. Since she was in training for a triathlon, she borrowed Jim's bike and asked me to join her for a ride. I kept up with her for about ten miles, and fell behind when my rickety old legs starting cramping. It wasn't the distance that was the problem; it was the speed. She charged down the bike trail disappearing for several minutes, and then returning to check on me. Once I slowed my pace I was able to complete twenty miles and meet up with her. At that point the bike path entered a heavily forested area and a sign said: "Beware of hunters." We decided that if there was a bike trail it must be safe, but we soon learned otherwise. A few minutes later we heard gunshots, and then shortly thereafter a fellow in camouflage clothing with a rifle slung over his back came pedaling toward us. My immediate thought was to turn around to avoid a stray bullet. Every hunting season there were reports of a hunter seeing a movement and shooting only to find that he had killed another hunter, not a deer.

After we turned around we still had twenty miles to go to return to our starting place. The return ride was a lonely one as my daughter continued at her usual pace and left me gasping and groaning and trudging along many miles behind her. I couldn't help but think about the hunter. If he were truly expecting to bag a deer, just where was he planning to put the carcass on his bike? While I was contemplating this, my daughter returned to tell me to hurry up. She suggested I use her "ferris wheel" racing technique to improve my speed. I had tried it once before when going through those tunnels along the Columbia

Dare To Do It!

River. It didn't have much effect then, and it didn't improve my technique now. My "ferris wheel" was clearly rusty and not likely to improve at my age.

Once the picnic was over and the relatives had gone home, Jim and I headed east across Wisconsin to Door County, a peninsula that stuck out into Lake Michigan. In order to access the area, we had to go through the town of Green Bay, the land of the Cheese Heads, the Packers. As we drove through the center of town we noticed that almost every structure was painted green and gold. We even passed an Amish fellow whose carriage was painted the Packer colors. These people took their football seriously.

After leaving Green Bay we drove north up the western side of the peninsula where we began to see quaint little villages tucked along the shore. They had unusual names like Egg Harbor and Sister Bay. The naturally beauty of the area attracted tourists by the thousands and provided a thriving economy for local businesses. Since no one came in the wintertime, the proprietors had to find ways to attract the visitors to their establishments.

One restaurant had planted grass on its pitched roof and hauled up a bunch of goats. People flocked around the building searching for the perfect photo. I took a couple of pictures, wondering as I did so, if any of the goats ever stumbled and fell off. At night when it was dark, kids being kids, a young one could easily romp right off the edge. I checked out the restaurant's menu offerings: no goat.

One day we made reservations for a famous boiled fish dinner. After signing in we were directed out to the back of the restaurant to sit on logs or tree stumps in a forested clearing. In the middle of the area was a huge cauldron sitting on a wood fire. After all the guests had arrived and were seated, a man came out of the restaurant and told funny stories while he dropped fish into the boiling oil. After he finished speaking, he dumped kerosene onto the fire causing flames to shoot some thirty to forty feet into the air. This was the dramatic ending to story hour. We then returned to the restaurant where a waitress deboned and drizzled melted butter over the fish. Boiling made the fish ever so tender and the butter gave it a wonderful taste. Veggies that had also been boiled in the oil were served as well, and the meal ended when everyone was served cherry pie made from local fruit.

Away from the coastline the roads throughout the peninsula were quiet country lanes that were perfect for biking. We didn't see the water because we were too far inland, but we didn't see any tourists either. Wisconsin roads are labeled with alphabet letters. I thought that was strange since the letters were not in order. If we biked Road Q, we would expect the next road over to be Road R, but that was not the case. I wondered if people got confused if there was a Road Q and a Road O. Apparently the system worked, it was just confusing to me.

It was now the middle of September and the weather was perfect: sunshine and high temperatures. But still in the backs of our minds we knew that as we traveled north the weather could quickly turn cold and rainy. We had brought rain jackets with us, but at our ages the last thing we wanted to do was to be cycling with water dripping off our helmets and splashing on our exposed legs. We decided it was time to leave Door County and head up into Canada.

We cycled north along Lake Michigan to Sault St. Marie, crossed over into Canada and then headed southeast towards Toronto. We followed our usual daily routine, biking in the late mornings and early afternoons and then finding a hotel where Jim could take his nap and I could work on the computer. The shoulder of the roads was adequate and the land fairly level, and with light traffic we could relax and enjoy the biking without the stress of vehicles causing us to quake and quiver at their approach.

As we biked south through heavily forested areas, we sometimes encountered swarms of insects that hung in the air like huge black balloons. The swarms seemed to appear out of nowhere and once we were enveloped, millions of them would be flying every which way, stinging arms and legs, crawling up noses and ears and tiptoeing across goggles. Just when it seemed as if I would go crazy from the bombardment, the mass would suddenly disappear. The extraordinary number of bugs caused me to instinctively shut my mouth. That was an obvious reaction. But that was not always the case.

Once when I forgot to keep my mouth closed, a bug swooped in landing in the back of my mouth. I coughed and cleared my throat and tried, in vain, to spit the damn thing out. It tickled my throat, it clung to my tonsils, and it churned its little feet thrashing back and forth. But no matter how much I tried to expel it, the insect lost its hold and down my esophagus it went in a creepy crawly dance to certain death. Even though I knew that stomach acids would have immediately dissolved the bug, I could feel the tickle in my throat for several hours. I never could understand how a single insect, that could go wherever it chose, would be on a flight path that led directly to my mouth. After that first experience I vowed to keep my mouth shut.

Traveling through Ontario Province turned out to be exactly as we had originally envisioned our biking experience would be. We found a low traffic road that either ran along the shore of the Saint Lawrence River or inland just a couple of miles. If we were near the river we enjoyed dazzling views of the sun dancing across the water. At the same time, we had to contend with strong winds whose gusts often made us feel as if we were air borne. It seemed that nothing good could be gained without effort. We struggled along, exhausted from going short distances, while we looked at the beautiful scenery.

On one of those days combating the wind and pushing ourselves along, we saw in an unusual sight in the river. A medieval castle appeared to be floating in the middle of the Saint Lawrence. Intrigued, we stopped at a nearby village and from our questions we learned that a man named George Boldt had built the Bavarian-style castle for his wife. She died before she and George could move in, and so, Boldt left the castle empty where it fell into ruin. In the 1970s the castle was renovated and turned into a tourist attraction. After inquiring about taking a tour, we learned that most boat trips had stopped running for the season, but one boat would be making a special trip the next day to accommodated a busload of foreign tourists passing through the area.

Since we had to wait until the next day, we had to find lodging. The one hotel near the boat landing was unavailable, but we were directed down the road to a small motel tucked away in the woods at the end of a dead end road. Because the tourist season was finished, the motel was empty, but the owner, who lived on site, agreed to rent us a room. The motel was very plain and would have blended into the woods if it were not for the bright orange-red doors. When we asked about the unusual color, the owner explained that the color symbolized good luck to the Chinese, and so he hoped that some rich Chinese person would offer him a million dollars in cash. He said that a Chinese man had driven up to his neighbor's farm and offered to purchase the place for a million dollars. The motel owner hoped to be just as lucky.

The next day Jim and I went to the boat landing ready to take our tour. We had hoped to leave that morning so that after the hour-long tour we could continue cycling up the river. We waited for several hours, and just when we thought the tour would be cancelled, a bus arrived and out spilled a group of young Russians, all newlyweds. As soon as they climbed aboard the boat we took off.

The boat circled the castle and then motored through several islands where we saw mansions, some similar to those in Newport, Rhode Island. We learned that, in fact, most of the structures were summer homes built by East Coast millionaires. All of the houses were in U.S. waters including the castle. That meant that during the tourist season when boats stopped at the castle, visitors had to have a passport to step on the island. On one tiny island the house had a sign posted indicating that the house was in Canada, but the boat dock was in the United States. Since the homes were large and the islands small, Jim and I wondered if the occupants had plumbing, electricity and drinking water.

While Jim and I looked at the practicalities of living on the islands, the Russian couples had squeezed themselves into nooks and crannies snuggling and smooching. They had no interest in the scenery outside the boat windows. When the boat returned to the dock, the honeymooners quickly left the boat, climbed into the bus and disappeared. Jim and I still had a few hours that afternoon to cycle. Taking time for the tour was a nice diversion, but we kept worrying about the weather. The further north we went the greater the chance the weather would change.

We continued up the Saint Lawrence enjoying beautiful surroundings. For several days we simply enjoyed biking without worrying about traffic. Along the way we came to the Long Sault Parkway, a series of islands connected by bridges situated in the middle of the river. With only a few fishermen sitting under the bridges, we had the place to ourselves. The sunny weather and the quiet roadway made for ideal biking. We would have stayed much longer, but it was almost the end of September and we still had a long way to go.

When we reached Quebec Province, we found the cycling extremely stressful. There were no bike paths, and shoulders on the roadways were narrow. Vehicles traveled at breakneck speeds completely oblivious to cyclists. Biking so close to the traffic was frightening. The cacophony of honking, the thick black exhaust and the draft from oversized trucks made this part of our trip a nightmare. We had not encountered such hazardous traffic since leaving Washington and Oregon State.

By the time we approached Montreal, the biking had become so treacherous that we could not continue on the direct approach to the city. We turned off and tried to cycle around on the outskirts, but the urban sprawl was so extensive that we ended passing by the city without a glimpse. It appeared that every road was under construction. We cycled a couple of miles and then had to climb in the car and drive through craters where bulldozers had dug up the earth. Trying to negotiate the construction areas, we crept along at five miles per hour. Apparently, that was too slow for the drivers behind us, for they would gesture out their windows indicating that they wanted us to go faster, and as soon as we reached pavement, would speed pass us yelling expletives.

It took over five hours to bypass Montreal. A local told us that there are only two seasons in Quebec Province: winter season and construction season. After Montreal every five or six miles we came to a dead stop because of road repairs. When we crept along the dirt track, the cars in front of us sent up clouds of dirt that engulfed our car causing visibility to literally disappear. Turning on the windshield wipers just pushed the dirt around and when Jim sprayed the windows with water the muddy mixture often obscured the outside so that Jim had to open the window to see where to drive. This caused choking dirt to fill the interior of the car. When we had passed the construction areas and the impatient French drivers had disappeared, we would sigh with relief, and try to ride our bikes for the short distance to the next construction site.

After we left the environs of Montreal the traffic had increased dramatically and the roads had morphed into giant freeways, so that biking into Quebec City looked totally unsafe. After examining a map of the province, we found some local roads that headed out of the city to the north where the biking would be reasonably safe due to the smaller roads. With that plan in mind, we drove into the city to find our hotel. That proved to be a challenge.

Quebec City sits on a huge rocky pinnacle with the old town of cobblestone streets sloping away from the rock face. The narrow streets are picturesque but certainly not built for the tour buses that were trying to negotiate them. To turn a corner a bus had to stop, back up, inch forward, back up, inch forward and so forth. And because the streets were so narrow, all of them had been turned into one-way lanes. So, when we tried to find our accommodations, we had to drive around in circles dodging buses and horse carriages and taxis.

When we finally found the hotel, there was only a short unloading zone. As soon as we stopped, young men quickly threw open the doors and started hauling our belonging into the lobby. Jim and I had piled all of our equipment and clothing into storage bins. It was a bit embarrassing when we enter the lobby and saw everything strewn about the floor in front of the reception desk. We had decided to stay in an old world hotel, and this place fit the description, but it was not set up to accommodate people like us. Visitors going in and out of the hotel had to stumble around our bikes and the bins. When we asked for a dolly so that we could get everything picked up, the bellboys waved us off. The concierge assured us that our belongings were safe, and in the meantime he would escort us to our room. It was a good thing he did, or we would have been lost.

We rode the elevator to the top floor of the hotel where the concierge led us up and down narrow corridors often interspersed with four or five stairs going up and then after turning a corner, four or five stairs going down. We went this way and that and by the time we arrive at our room we had no idea where we actually were in the hotel. My first thought was that if there were a fire we would never be able to find our way out of the maze. The room was quite small as is typical of old world European style hotels. It was even a bit claustrophobic because the tiny window, located high on one wall, let in very little light. I had to stand on a chair to look out, and then all I could see were the rooftops of nearby buildings and a tiny sliver of sky between chimneys. This must be what the French called a garret. We were clearly in the attic.

The bellboys arrived, and, by the time they stacked our bins and found room for our bikes, we had only the space on the bed. We had to crawl over the bed to get to the bathroom. After we freshened up and decided to go out to dinner, we spent at least twenty minutes of trial and error wandering the narrow corridors until we finally found an elevator to take us to the lobby. We had a delicious dinner at a restaurant recommended by one of the bellboys, and didn't realize, until later, that that would end up being the only decent meal we had in the city.

Quebec City in the late fall was still inundated with tourists. We had planned to bike along the base of the rock and then north out of town, but the massive number of tourists flowing back and forth across the main roadway was discouraging. They stopped in the middle of the street oblivious to the traffic and the drivers honking and cursing at them. But who can blame them. They had just debarked from their cruise ships, and, looking up, the first thing they would see would be Le Chateau Frontenac, the turreted hotel that had become the iconic symbol of the city. The only place where one could take a photograph that included the bronze roof and the front of the hotel was from the base of the rocky pinnacle.

Nearby adhering to the bottom of the rock was the oldest street in Quebec. Only a few blocks long, its cobbled paving lined with old world buildings dating back hundreds of years could not have been lovelier. But to see it, we had to get up a daybreak when the tourists were still tucked into their berths on the ships or in beds in high-end hotels. Once the city woke up, the souvenir stands and advertising signage spilled out into the street completely obscuring the picturesque architecture.

Somehow the city managed to maintain the French ambiance despite the flood of tourists, who wandered in and out of souvenir shops, examining the wares that were all the same from one place to the next. The streets became so crowded that the people appeared to flitter like flocks of birds, moving in waves from one spot to another, settling down for a few minutes, only to move again en mass.

To accommodate the tourists, who apparently had no interest in exercise, the city fathers had installed an elevator so one could ride to the top of the rock or down to the waterfront. There was a stairway, but few people were on it.

On top of the rock and in front of the Le Chateau Frontenac was a large promenade where one could look out at the river. That is, one could enjoy a view of the river if it weren't for the huge cruise ships that blocked the view. At the entrance to the lovely hotel Le Chateau was a Starbucks sign. It would have been more aesthetically pleasing if the city fathers had restricted the sign to one that complemented the hotel rather than the garish neon one that besmirched the building.

Trying to maintain the French atmosphere and still accommodate all the tourists had to be a difficult problem for Quebec City. Besides the two or three cruise ships that were berthed on the waterfront, Jim and I counted fourteen tour buses parked on the street next to the Chateau hotel. We had visited the city years ago and remembered the quaint little bakery on one corner and the tiny drug store on another. All of that had disappeared. Besides souvenir shops, there were ice cream parlors and candy stores. Apparently that is what tourists purchase when on vacation.

We stayed in the city for two days and visited a couple of places on the outskirts of the old town, and we tried eating a meal in one of the outdoor tourist cafes, but the rushed service and the poor quality of food just added to our impressions of a place that we no longer recognized. There were musicians, who played French songs; mimes who stood motionless for hours; and drivers taking people about in horse drawn carriages. The tourists were happy. But this city was a perfect example of a dilemma that affects all tourist attractions. A place is discovered because of its unique qualities. But then, the tourists come in droves overwhelming the local facilities, and what attracted the people there in the first place simply disappears.

Many countries are now banning tourists from certain attractions in order to keep the places from being ruined. The French closed the Lascaux Caves and built a replica for tourists. Perhaps that will be the answer in the future.

Tired of the crowds, we happily left Quebec City behind and headed across the Saint Lawrence to begin cycling up the southern bank of the river. When we had driven this route back in the seventies, we had found quaint little villages dotting the coastline. In each village the elderly inhabitants had constructed outdoor ovens that looked just like beehives. After stopping to purchase some of the bakery products that came out of those ovens, we discovered they were the most delicious food we had ever eaten. We agreed that the baked goods were worth a return trip. However, we never made it back. Now as we biked through the villages, we looked for those delectable treats again. Sadly, the beehive ovens were history. Our queries were met with blank stares. No one knew what we were talking about.

We cycled through the tiny villages along the coast enjoying stress-free biking because there was no traffic. People heading to the Gaspe Peninsula now traveled on a new inland highway that was much faster since they did not have to slow down to go through any towns. North of the villages we came to the town of Rimouski, the gateway to the Gaspe. Most visitors stayed here, taking day trips into the forested peninsula. The area offered trails for hiking and biking in the great outdoors.

After our usual cycling routine, we checked into a hotel in Rimouski. When we had unloaded all of our gear and headed back to the car to lock up, we discovered a flat tire. It seemed that this might be a big problem since our rudimentary French did not include vocabulary involving tires, but Jim was able to find a solution when he asked the concierge to write down the problem in French, and Jim simply took the note to the repair shop and had the tire fixed right away. We had covered four thousand miles on our bikes and in our car and had only two flats on our bikes and one on our car. We felt very lucky.

After a day relaxing and enjoying the town, we began the last leg of our journey. Traveling up the northern coast along the peninsula, we rarely saw any traffic even though there was only the one road that encircled the peninsula starting and ending in Rimouski. We passed small clusters of weather worn structures clinging to the rocky coast. Some were on stilts that leaned so much to one side that it seemed as if we would see one fall into the ocean. Perhaps the reason they looked so lonely and forlorn is that we never saw any inhabitants. If there were people living there they had to be hardy souls to stand the ferocious wind that continuously blew. As the land curved southward, the wind became brutal.

At this point we recognized that we had reached our goal of cycling from the Pacific to the Atlantic. We had wanted to continue biking to the small town of Gaspe or to Perce before feeling satisfied that we had completed our goal, but that was not to be. The wind was so strong that we could not stand up without holding on to the car, so trying to bike had become impossible. I had tried to cycle using the car as a shield but Jim just keep nagging me to give it up. I had to admit I was barely able to stay on the bike and then, instead of going forward, I felt as if I were going backwards. After thirty minutes I was exhausted and had to quit in defeat. Even securing the bike to the back of the car was a major operation as the bike was light and the wind could have easily picked it up and thrown it away. Still, it was sunny and warm.

Just as we had secured the bikes on the car and began driving down the road, we came to a huge dip whose sides appeared to be almost vertical. As we cautiously drove down into its depths, we saw a remarkable sight. Here was a man pedaling the incline zigzagging up while his handlebars appeared to be scraping the sides of the road. We waved encouragement knowing that what he was doing was well beyond our abilities.

Dare To Do It!

Were it not for the narrow beach and the sun shining off the water, the heavily forested land that bordered the road on the inland side looked dark and dreary. Peeking out from the tops of the trees were hundreds of wind turbines. They reminded me of the novel, *The Day of the Triffids*, in which enormous plants attempted to take over the earth. The way that some blades were spinning quickly, other moving slowly, and still others standing perfectly still suggested mechanical monsters that could communicate with each other. Jim and I were happy to move south around the peninsula where the land was more open and welcoming.

We drove through the village of Gaspe and then on to Perce where we decided to spend the night. The little town has built several hotels to accommodate the summer crowds, who come to photograph a massive rock formation that sits close to shore. When the wind-whipped waves crash through a blowhole at he end of the rock, the spray creates dramatic patterns that change with sunlight.

The next day we decided to continue biking even though we had already accomplished our goal. With less wind and lots of sunshine we found the southern edge of the Gaspe perfect for cycling. Before we left Perce, we stopped for a cup of coffee, and, much to our surprise, saw pictures of those beehive ovens on the walls of the shop. When we asked the owner about the ovens, he said they no longer existed. Except for the pictures, the old world baking ovens were ancient history.

Our plans to bike that day were quickly quashed. Not five miles down the road we ran into a construction site. The road was torn up so that only a single dirt track continued on. The road had been devoid of traffic, and now we understood why. At least ten cars were sitting in line waiting for a traffic light to turn green. When the light had not changed after fifteen minutes the first car took off, and the rest of us followed. As soon as the car tires touched pavement, the drivers gunned their engines and flew down the road leaving us alone.

Jim wanted to get away from the dirty dust-filled air before stopping so that I could unload my bike and ride, but we had not gone more than a couple of miles when we came to another construction site. We waited in line again until the first car took off, ignoring the red stoplight, and negotiated the narrow one lane track until reaching pavement again. We drove through several more construction sites with the same scenario until finally arriving back at Rimouski.

After a night in Rimouski, we started back down the peninsula stopping to take turns cycling. Jim only went out for a short spin because he said the wind made it too difficult to bike. Feeling enthusiastic about the continued fine weather, I decided I had to get out on my bike. The new highway running south from Rimouski to Quebec City was bordered by farmland devoid of trees and that meant there was nothing to block the wind coming off the river. As soon as I got out of the car I felt the wind hitting me with tremendous force. It was not as intense as what we had encountered on the Gaspe, but it was strong enough to make pedaling extremely difficult. With high temperatures and sunshine it seemed a shame to give up cycling just because of the wind. I pushed my legs up and down making my bike move forward, but it was so slow I barely kept upright. After an hour I had only completed a mile. I had to quit. The wind was just too powerful.

Both Jim and I were feeling so good with the warm sunny weather we wanted to continue our journey as long as we could. There was something supremely satisfying about completing a set number of miles each day. It was October, and early mornings and late evenings were filled with arctic air. Jim started his cycling later in the morning to avoid the chill. Now that we were headed west toward home, we had to think about traveling over the passes in the Rocky Mountains and whether we would encounter snow. With that in mind we decided to drive the freeways, stopping early enough in the afternoons so that we could bike a couple of hours on quiet roads near the Interstate. It wasn't long before we had retraced our bike tracks down the Saint Lawrence, across Ontario Province and into the United States.

Once back in America, we headed north up the Michigan Peninsula and took a ferry to Mackinac Island. The weather was still perfect, so we decided to take one day to explore this famous attraction in the middle of Lake Huron. We tried to put our concerns about crossing the Rockies out of our minds so we could enjoy the tiny island. Even at this late time of year, the place was jammed packed with tourists. We were attracted to the island because it was famous for its ban on motorized vehicles, only allowing horse drawn carriages and bicycles. The road along the perimeter of the island hugged the beach and provided unparalleled views of the lake.

The one and only town was photogenic with its pristine white buildings decorated with bouquets of colorful flowers spilling from every window. To add to the ambiance one only had to walk a couple of blocks to find dramatic waves crashing against the rocky shore. Most of the tourists stayed in the urban area checking out the usual souvenir shops and eating in the many restaurants tucked into every corner of every alley. Once Jim and I were able to negotiate through the crowds and find the road encircling the island, our cycling was pleasant and peaceful sharing the road with only a handful of other cyclists. But the rest of the island was just too touristy to be enjoyable.

Dare To Do It!

I had anticipated a place of unquestionable beauty because plenty of people we knew had been to Mackinac Island and raved about it. But perhaps I needed rose-tinted glasses, or maybe I needed to look less carefully at details. I assumed the horse-drawn carriages would be like those prancing around Central Park in New York City, but these carriages were flatbed trailers sitting on large truck tires. With benches lined up to hold some ten to fifteen people, there was no feeling of privacy or romantic intimacy unless one counted the elbow of a stranger digging into one's side. It looked as if the loads were too much for the tired horses, and I looked away whenever a carriage approached. Every time we completed a circuit of the island and had to negotiate our way through the crowds, we found ourselves getting more frustrated. It was time for us to catch the next ferry and return to the mainland.

We traveled across Wisconsin on the freeways and then stopped in Minnesota to ride several of the northern bike trails we had not been on before. These bike trails were in heavily forested areas where the fall colors were in full glory. Trees formed canopies overhead with colorful leaves in brilliant reds, yellows and gold. It was unbelievably beautiful.

We continued heading west on the Interstate across North Dakota and Montana. Neither state had any bike trails that interested us, so we headed up into the Rockies. As soon as we left Missoula it began to snow. It got heavier and thicker and covered the highway. With no chains and no winter clothes to put on if we went into a ditch, we inched along until we finally reached the top of Lookout Pass. Once on the other side, the snow suddenly disappeared, the sun shone brightly, and the road was bare. We drove down into Coeur d'Alene, Idaho completely exhausted from the tension of worrying about the road conditions. We decided to stay the night.

The next morning we awoke to warm sunny skies next to gorgeous Lake Coeur d'Alene. With bike trails all along the lake edge we knew we had to stay a couple of days to take advantage of the weather. When we finally left Idaho, it only took a few hours for us to reach our home near Puget Sound in Washington State. It was good to be home but a bit of a let down after the routine of cycling every day. It was time to return to the reality of our daily lives.

It has been a couple of years since our "great adventure," and each summer when we talk about making a similar trip, we have found the weather to be uncooperative. Eastern Washington has had many forest fires, and the Midwest has experienced an unusual number of tornadoes and hailstorms. We still hope to take more cycling trips in the future as long as we are able, but, as we grow older, we know that the length of the trips will have to be shorter. We also continue to visit different parts of the world seeking adventure.

Idaho was one of our favorite places because of the beautiful scenery.

Dare To Do It!

Jim at the top of Rogers Pass.

Jim and Nancy in Montana.

Dare To Do It!

Prop used in the movie, "Fargo".

Paddle wheeler on the Mississippi River.

Dare To Do It!

Bike art.

Nancy Rubesch

Goats on the roof are a local attraction in Door County, WI.

Dare To Do It!

Boldt Castle sitting in the middle of the Saint Lawrence River

Chateau Frontenac, a famous landmark, in Quebec City, Quebec, Canada.

Dare To Do It!

Autumn foliage on bike path in Minnesota.

www.ingramcontent.com/pod-product-compliance
Lightning Source LLC
Chambersburg PA
CBHW071729080526
44588CB00013B/1956